The Timelessness of Proust
Reflections on *In Search of Lost Time*

Other Books of Interest from St. Augustine's Press

Wayne J. Hankey, *Aquinas's Neoplatonism in the Summa Theologiae on God: A Short Introduction*

Karl Rahner, S.J., *Ignatius of Loyola Speaks*

St. Augustine, *The St. Augustine LifeGuide: Words to Live by from the Great Christian Saint*

James V. Schall, *The Regensburg Lecture*

John of Saint Thomas, *Introduction to the Summa Theologiae of Thomas Aquinas*

Jean-Luc Marion, *Descartes's Grey Ontology*

Richard Watson, *Descartes's Ballet*

Richard Watson, *The Philosopher's Enigma: God, Body & Soul*

Theo Verbeek, *Descartes and the Dutch: Early Reactions to Cartesian Philosophy 1637–1650*

Leszek Kolakowski, *Religion If There Is No God . . .*

Leszek Kolakowski, *Husserl and the Search for Certitude*

Catherine O'Neil and Zbigniew Janowski, *Juliusz Slowacki's Agamemnon's Tomb: A Polish Oresteia*

Zbigniew Janowski, *How to Read Descartes's Meditations*

Zbigniew Janowski, *Augustinina-Cartesian Index: Text and Commentary*

Stanley Rosen, *The Ancients and the Moderns*

Emanuela Scribano, *A Reading Guide to Descartes's Meditations on First Philosophy*

Rémi Brague, *Moderately Modern*

Roger Pouivet, *After Wittgenstein, St. Thomas*

H. S. Gerdil, *The Anti-Emile: Reflections on the Theory and Practice of Education against the Principles of Rousseau*

Celia Wolf-Devine, *Descartes on Seeing: Epistemology and Visual Perception*

The Timelessness of Proust
Reflections on *In Search of Lost Time*

Edited by Charles R. Embry
& Glenn Hughes

ST. AUGUSTINE'S PRESS
South Bend, Indiana

Manufactured in the United States of America.

1 2 3 4 5 6   25 24 23 22 21 20 19

Library of Congress Cataloging in Publication Data
Names: Embry, Charles R., 1942– editor.
Hughes, Glenn, 1951– editor.
Title: The timelessness of Proust : reflections on a search of lost time /
edited by Charles R. Embry and Glenn Hughes.
Description: South Bend, Indiana : St. Augustine's Press, 2016.
Includes bibliographical references.
Identifiers: LCCN 2016012550
ISBN 9781587318634 (paperbound : alk. paper)
Subjects: LCSH: Proust, Marcel, 1871–1922.
À la recherche du temps perdu.
Proust, Marcel, 1871-1922--Criticism and interpretation.
Classification: LCC PQ2631.R63 A925 2016 I DDC 843/.912--dc23
LC record available at https://lccn.loc.gov/2016012550

∞ The paper used in this publication meets the minimum
requirements of the American National Standard for Information Sciences -
Permanence of Paper for Printed Materials, ANSI Z39.48-1984.

St. Augustine's Press
www.staugustine.net

This book is dedicated to the memory of Thomas A. Hollweck.

Table of Contents

Introduction
Charles R. Embry

This book of six essays is unique in exploring Marcel Proust's novel *In Search of Lost Time* through the illuminative lens of the philosophical thought of Eric Voegelin. Five of these essays were originally presented at a roundtable panel entitled "The Timelessness of Proust," which I organized and chaired for the 2014 Eric Voegelin Society program at the annual meeting of the American Political Science Association in Washington, D.C. The sixth essay, written by Glenn Hughes, extended his work for that panel to compare themes common in Proust's novel and T. S. Eliot's *Four Quartets*.

The reader may well ask: what relevance does Voegelin's philosophy have for the examination and interpretation of Proust's masterpiece?

First, Voegelin's philosophical search of order over his lifetime, expressed in the thirty-four volumes of his *Collected Works*, focused not only on works of philosophy, political science, law, etc., but also on numerous works that have traditionally been categorized as literature. For example, he read and analyzed classic ancient texts such as Homer, Hesiod, the Greek dramatists, the Bible, and Hindu writings. Beyond that, and importantly, he often drew on modern literary authors both to explain his philosophical vision and to develop his diagnosis and critique of modernity, with special attention paid to works of Shakespeare, Flaubert, Baudelaire, Henry James, Thomas Mann, T. S. Eliot, Robert Musil, Heimito von Doderer, Cervantes, and Proust.[1]

---

1   Voegelin's interest in philosophical anthropology led him to study literary works of almost every genre. In a 1956 letter to his friend Robert B. Heilman, a literary critic and historian of literature, he asserted that "[t]he occupation with works of art, poetry, philosophy, mythical imagination, and so forth, makes sense only, if it is conducted as an inquiry into the nature

From time to time—primarily in his correspondence with fellow scholars and friends—Voegelin would write extended comments on a particular literary work. For example, he wrote a long letter to Robert B. Heilman in which he reviewed a book manuscript of Heilman's on *King Lear*. Some of his observations and suggestions were incorporated by Heilman into the book that grew from the manuscript reviewed by Voegelin, *This Great Stage: Image and Structure in* King Lear.[2] Some time later, after Heilman had sent a copy to Voegelin of an article he'd written on Henry James's *Turn of the Screw*, Voegelin responded with a long letter analyzing the novella. This letter, first written in 1947,[3] was later published together with a "Postscript" in 1971 by *Southern Review*.[4]

of man. That sentence, while it excludes historicism, does not exclude history, for it is peculiar to the nature of man that it unfolds its potentialities historically. Not that historically anything 'new' comes up—human nature is always wholly present—but there are modes of clarity and degrees of comprehensiveness in man's understanding of his self and his position in the world." Charles R. Embry, ed. with Introduction, Foreword by Champlin B. Heilman, *Robert B. Heilman and Eric Voegelin: A Friendship in Letters, 1944–1984* (Columbia: University of Missouri Press, 2004), 157. Those who are interested in exploring how the elements of Voegelin's philosophy pertain to literature may especially consult Letters 9, 11, 65, and 103 in this volume, and Charles R. Embry, *The Philosopher and the Storyteller: Eric Voegelin and Twentieth-Century Literature* (Columbia: University of Missouri Press, 2008). Lewis P. Simpson, in "Voegelin and the Story of the Clerks," relates Voegelin's work to the European tradition of literature; see Ellis Sandoz, *Eric Voegelin's Significance for the Modern Mind* (Baton Rouge: Louisiana State University Press, 1991), 71–110. For those who wish to read how Voegelin's philosophical work aids in understanding literature and art generally, I suggest *A More Beautiful Question: The Spiritual in Poetry and Art* (Columbia: University of Missouri Press, 2011), in which Glenn Hughes explores literary and artistic works within a philosophical context informed by the work of Voegelin and Bernard Lonergan.

2   Letter 9 in Embry, *A Friendship in Letters*, 31–37.
3   Letter 11 in Embry, *A Friendship in Letters*, 39–52.
4   *Southern Review*, New Series, VII, 1, 3-48 (1971). Voegelin's original letter and the "Postscript: On Paradise and Revolution" were published as "On Henry James's *Turn of the Screw*," in Eric Voegelin, *Published Essays, 1966–1985*, vol. 12 of *The Collected Works of Eric Voegelin*, ed. with Introduction by Ellis Sandoz (Columbia: University of Missouri Press, 1990), 134–71.

The Postscript to his *Turn of the Screw* letter afforded Voegelin the opportunity to raise an important principle of his approach to literary criticism: the inclusion of "the existential structure" of a work of literature into a critical analysis of that work. One of his more extensive and explicit statements on literary criticism addressing this topic appears in a letter to Donald E. Stanford, coeditor of *Southern Review* when the *Turn of the Screw* letter and its Postscript were published. Commenting on a Wallace Stevens poem, "The Course of a Particular," that Stanford had sent him, Voegelin wrote:

> In spite of my admiration for the formal qualities of the poem I have certain misgivings about it. They are concerned with a subject matter that came up on the splendid evening of our discussion here in Stanford. On that occasion you stressed very strongly that the formal quality of a work of art is the one and only quality a literary critic has to take into account. And, if I remember correctly, I expressed equally strongly the opinion that in a critical judgment there must also be taken into account the existential content . . . .
>
> Most felicitously you characterize in your letter the poem as an expression of "the failure of transcendence." That is my point of resistance. The experience of a failure of transcendence is indeed expressed by the poem, but a failure of transcendence is no less a failure if it is expressed with poetic perfection. That is not an argument directed against Stevens especially. I would have to use it exactly in the same manner against Nietzsche and Heidegger, or Hegel. A "failure of transcendence" does not mean the transcendence has failed, but that something is existentially wrong with the man who is the victim of such failure.

* * *

I do not want to go further because, I think, the point I want to make has become clear; the fundamental question of literary criticism, whether the existential structure of the poem

should be included in the analysis of a work or not. Person-
ally, I think it must be included. There is a difference of quality of existence between, say, Aeschylus and Menander. . . .[5]

One sees from such comments that Voegelin's philosophical mind was
sharply attuned to the deepest meanings and resources of literature, and
can gather why his philosophies of consciousness and human existence
provide an excellent basis for its analysis.

Second, Voegelin maintained a long relationship with Proust's masterpiece that extended back to 1927 when he spent a year in Paris, at the
age of 26, as a Laura Spellman Rockefeller Memorial Scholar.[6] He re-
ported to Ellis Sandoz, who recorded his "autobiographical reflections,"
that "I acquired in this year in Paris a practically complete set of the important French prose literature from *La Princess de Clèves* by Madame
de La Fayette to the work of Marcel Proust, whose last volumes of *À la
recherche du temps perdu* were coming out at the time."[7]

Although in his published work Voegelin never systematically addressed Proust, at several places in his letters as well as in published essays he made tantalizing comments that indicate the continued
importance he attached to Proust's novel. Shortly after his year in Paris,
for example, Voegelin referenced Proust several times in a 1928 essay
on the Declaration of the Rights of Man and Citizen.[8] In a 1945 letter in

5 Eric Voegelin, Letter 357, in Voegelin, *Selected Correspondence, 1950–1984*, vol. 30 of *The Collected Works of Eric Voegelin*, translations from the German by Sandy Adler, Thomas A. Hollweck, and William Petropulos, ed. with Introduction by Thomas A. Hollweck (Columbia: University of Missouri Press), 665–66.
6 Eric Voegelin, *Autobiographical Reflections: Revised Edition with a Voegelin Glossary and Cumulative Index*, vol. 34 of *The Collected Works of Eric Voegelin*, ed. with Introduction by Ellis Sandoz (Columbia: University of Missouri Press, 2006), 34.
7 Ibid., 35.
8 Eric Voegelin, "The Meaning of the Declaration of the Rights of Man and Citizen of 1789," in Voegelin, *Published Essays, 1922–1928*, vol. 7 of *The Collected Works of Eric Voegelin*, tr. M. J. Hanak, ed. with Introduction by Thomas W. Heilke and John von Heyking (Columbia: University of Missouri Press, 2003), 285–335.

which he discusses the work of his friend Alfred Schütz, he closes with a paragraph that surveys a number of interesting questions to Schütz arising from the latter's manuscript. Among these he includes: "[F]or example, how would you deal with the certainly meaningful experiences that make up the structure of Proust's *Recherche du temps perdu?*"[9] Three years later, when he was working on Plato's *Laws* for *Plato and Aristotle*, the third volume of his magnum opus *Order and History*, Voegelin wrote to Willmoore Kendall that "what fascinated me particularly about this last work of Plato was the literary form which has certain resemblances to Proust's *Recherche*."[10] And in 1964, thirty-seven years after he first read the last volumes of *Recherche*, Proust still occupied a place in Voegelin's thinking. At this time he was working on his book *Anamnesis*, one of his most significant contributions to the philosophy of consciousness. In a letter of that year he explained to Robert Heilman what he meant by what he had come to call "The Time of the Tale."

> There was a point in my Salzburg lecture that might interest you as an historian of literature: The basic form of myth, the "tale" in the widest sense, including the epic as well as the dramatic account of happenings, has a specific time, immanent to the tale, whose specific character consists in the ability to combine human, cosmic and divine elements into one story. I have called it, already in *Order and History*, the Time of the Tale. It expresses the experience of being (that embraces all sorts of reality, the cosmos) in flux. This Tale with its Time seems to me the primary literary form, peculiar to cosmological civilizations. Primary in the sense, that it precedes all literary form developed under conditions of differentiating experiences: If man becomes differentiated with any degree of autonomy from the cosmic context, then, and only

9   Letter 197 to Alfred Schütz, October 6, 1945, in Eric Voegelin, *Selected Correspondence, 1924–1949*, vol. 29 of *The Collected Works of Eric Voegelin*, trans. by William Petropulos, ed. with Introduction by Jürgen Gebhardt (Columbia: University of Missouri Press, 2009), 448.
10 Letter 252, ibid., 565.

then, will develop specifically human forms of literature: The story of human events, lyric, empirical history, the drama and tragedy of human action, the meditative dialogue in the Platonic sense, etc. Underlying all later, differentiated forms, however, there remains the basic Tale which expresses Being in flux. Time, then, would not be an empty container into which you can fill any content, but there would be as many times as there are types of differentiated content. Think for instance of Proust's *temps perdu* and *temps retrouvé* as times which correspond to the loss and rediscovery of self, the action of rediscovery through a monumental literary work of remembrance being the atonement for the loss of time through personal guilt—very similar to cosmological rituals of restoring order that has been lost through lapse of time.[11]

Finally, in 1977 Voegelin contributed a new "introductory" chapter to Gerhart Niemeyer's translation of *Anamnesis*[12] and entitled it "Remembrance of Things Past," an obvious allusion to the Moncrief English translation of *À la recherche du temps perdu*, which remained the standard English translation until the now widely accepted Modern Library translation, *In Search of Lost Time*. It is very significant that Voegelin chose this title, for it connects Voegelin's continuing interest in Proust to his late writings and meditations.

It seems clear that Voegelin's periodic comments on Proust's novel evidence an almost sixty-year concern with Proust's explorations of human consciousness; and in fact, the more I read and reflect on Voegelin's late work as well as on Proust's masterpiece, the more I am convinced that Voegelin's understanding of consciousness was greatly influenced by *À la recherche du temps perdu*. This is especially true, I believe, in his understanding of the importance of early childhood experiences in the developing trajectory of maturing consciousness. His "anamnetic experiments," first conducted in 1943, present evidence of

11 Letter 103 in Embry, *A Friendship in Letters*, 223.
12 Eric Voegelin, *Anamnesis*, translated and edited by Gerhart Niemeyer (Columbia, MO: University of Missouri Press, 1978), 3–13.

how childhood experiences "determine" the concerns of adult consciousness. He offered them for publication to the editor of *Sewanee Review* in 1946. In a letter to the editor, J. N. Palmer, Voegelin revealed how he thought of these experiments.

> If you would rather have something on the literary side, I have also lying around a MS entitled *Anamnesis*. It is an intellectual autobiography of my first ten years. The crazy thing originated in a correspondence with a friend on the question whether the Cartesian type of meditation is a legitimate approach to a philosophy of the mind. I denied the legitimacy on the ground that the life of the spirit and intellect is historical in the strict sense, and that the determinants of mature philosophical speculation have to be sought in the mythical formation of the mind in experiences of early youth. In order to prove my point, I made anamnetic experiments on myself and collected twenty-odd such early experiences which determined my later metaphysical attitudes.[13]

By 1966, however, when these anamnetic experiments were published in the German edition of *Anamnesis*, Voegelin's search of order—personal and collective—led to his interest in a philosophy of consciousness.[14] The literary nature of these experiments remained, but they had become a central element in his theory of the historical development of human consciousness.

The foregoing paragraphs have demonstrated not only Voegelin's familiarity with literature in general and the work of Proust, but also the

13 Letter to J. N. Palmer, November 5, 1946, Hoover Archives, Voegelin Papers, box 36, folder 8.
14 Gerhart Niemeyer, in the "Editor's Preface" (1977) to his translation of *Anamnesis*, commented that *Anamnesis* "shows the continuity of the hypothesis present from the moment in 1943 when Eric Voegelin, abandoning his project of a history of political ideas, turned to that work on consciousness as history and history as consciousness, the nexus construed ontologically rather than subjectively, idealistically, or psychologically . . . ." Voegelin, *Anamnesis*, Niemeyer, xxii.

importance of these in his philosophical search of order. But the aim of the following essays is to grapple with the masterpiece that is *In Search of Lost Time*, not to explain or interpret Voegelin's thought. The contributors—all of them quite familiar with Voegelin's work—have simply relied, sometimes overtly, sometimes implicitly, and sometimes obliquely, upon various dimensions of Voegelin's philosophical corpus to approach and analyze themes in Proust's novel.

My own essay explores how the novel can be read simultaneously as both *a* biography of consciousness, that of Proust's narrator Marcel, and (potentially) *the* biography of consciousness, i.e., that of his readers and indeed of Proust himself. Glenn Hughes, in "Proust, Transcendence, and Metaxic Existence," explores the correspondences and differences between Proust's and Voegelin's "literary vision" of existence in between time and timelessness, immanence and transcendence. Thomas J. McPartland contributes a "Philosophical Meditation on Proust's *In Search of Lost Time*," clarifying the meaning of his title by writing: "Given the nature of this masterpiece no commentary, literary or otherwise, can come close to doing it justice. If this is the case, a philosophical commentary must humbly take the form of a philosophical meditation. And even such a philosophical meditation can but be a simple philosophical invitation to participate in the work itself." Paulette Kidder reflects on "Imprisonment and Freedom" by focusing on the "long middle stretches" of the novel, in which "Marcel's epiphanic 'blessed impressions' seem all but forgotten," and wondering "how the parts of the novel" that she finds "most disquieting to read—those that chronicle Marcel's intense, controlling jealousy toward his lover Albertine and his continual mendacity toward her—can be integrated into a Voegelinian reading of the work." Michael Henry contributes another meditation on the novel, entitled "Proust's Luminous Memory and *L'Homme Éternel*: The Quest for Limitless Meaning," a meditation guided by his question: "What elevates such a semi-autobiographical novel to the rank of profoundly philosophical literature?" And in the final essay of the volume, "Unsought Revelations of Eternal Reality," Glenn Hughes examines the shared visions of human existence manifest in T. S. Eliot's *Four Quartets* and Proust's novel, specifically focusing on how both works portray human beings as capable of experiencing unexpected, mystical revelations of eternal meaning and how such experiences of timeless reality are always mediated through the "concrete realities of space and time."

We should, however, let the authors speak for themselves.

FINIS

Editorial Note

The authors collected here agreed to use the same edition of *In Search of Lost Time*. In order to facilitate shortened citations to this edition, I provide here the publication information to the edition that we used.

Marcel Proust, *In Search of Lost Time*, in 6 volumes, translated by C. K. Scott Moncrieff and Terence Kilmartin, revised by D. J. Enright, New York: Random House, The Modern Library Paperback Edition. 1999, 2003, 2004.

Specific volumes:

Volume I: *Swann's Way*, translated by C. K. Scott Moncrieff and Terence Kilmartin, revised by D. J. Enright. Introduction by Richard Howard. New York: Random House, The Modern Library Paperback Edition. 2004.

Volume II: *Within a Budding Grove*, translated by C. K. Scott Moncrieff and Terence Kilmartin, revised by D. J. Enright. New York: Random House, The Modern Library Paperback Edition. 2003.

Volume III: *The Guermantes Way*, translated by C. K. Scott Moncrieff and Terence Kilmartin, revised by D. J. Enright. New York: Random House, The Modern Library Paperback Edition. 2003.

Volume IV: *Sodom and Gomorrah*, translated by C. K. Scott Moncrieff and Terence Kilmartin, revised by D. J. Enright. New York: Random House, The Modern Library Paperback Edition. 2003.

Volume V: *The Captive* and *The Fugitive*, translated by C. K. Scott Moncrieff and Terence Kilmartin, revised by D. J. Enright. New York: Random House, The Modern Library Paperback Edition. 2003.

Volume VI: *Time Regained*, translated by Andreas Mayor and Terence Kilmartin, revised by D. J. Enright. With a Guide to Proust, compiled by Terence Kilmartin, revised by Joanna Kilmartin. New York: Random House, The Modern Library Paperback edition. 1999.

In Search of Lost Time:
Biographies of Consciousness
Charles R. Embry

For, in the past, nothing is irretrievably lost but everything is irrevocably stored. . . . Usually, to be sure, man considers only the stubble field of transitoriness and overlooks the full granaries of the past, wherein he had salvaged once and for all his deeds, his joys and also his sufferings.
—Viktor Frankl, *Man's Search for Meaning*

Eric Voegelin writes in the Foreword to *Anamnesis* that "consciousness is not a given to be deduced from outside but an experience of participation in the ground of being whose logos has to be brought to clarity through the meditative exegesis of itself."[1] In this book-length meditative exegesis, Voegelin establishes historical manifestations of "participation in the ground of being" in both the biography of the philosopher (Voegelin) and in the biography of humanity. In the chapter entitled "Anamnesis," he remembers the experiences in his own life that "opened sources of excitation, from which issue the urge to further philosophical reflection."[2] In the Prefatory Remarks to this chapter, Voegelin announces the assumptions that underlie the subsequent anamnetic experiments, remembrances from his childhood, in which he uncovers the roots of philosophizing in "the biography of philosophizing

1   Eric Voegelin, *Anamnesis: On the Theory of History and Politics*, vol. 6 of *The Collected Works of Eric Voegelin*, trans. M. J. Hanak based upon the abbreviated version originally translated by Gerhart Niemeyer, ed. with Introduction by David Walsh (Columbia, MO: University of Missouri Press, 2002), 33.
2   "Anamnesis" in Voegelin, *Anamnesis*, 85.

consciousness, i.e., by the experiences that impel toward reflection and do so because they have excited consciousness to the 'awe' of existence."[3] In my discussion of Proust's *In Search of Lost Time*, I rely upon three of these assumptions. To wit:

> (3) that the experiences of the transcendence of consciousness into the body, the external world, the community, history, and the ground of being are givens in *the biography of consciousness* and thus antecede the systematic reflection on consciousness; (4) that the systematic *reflection* operates with these experiences, or, at least, in its operations sets out from these experiences; that thus (5) the *reflection is a further event in the biography of consciousness* that may lead to clarification about its problems and, when *reflection* is turned in the direction of meditation, to the ascertainment of existence.[4]

I am not interested in demonstrating how these assumptions about consciousness are specifically applicable to an understanding of Proust's work, but rather in using them as parameters within which to reflect on *In Search of Lost Time*. More specifically I focus my attention on two phrases: "the biography of consciousness" and "reflection is a further event in the biography of consciousness." The first phrase provides my title and the second phrase permits me to talk about "events" in the biography of consciousness, for Voegelin's assertion that "reflection is a further event in the biography of consciousness" implies that the enumerated "experiences of the transcendence of consciousness" constitute events in the biography of consciousness.[5]

3   Ibid., 84.
4   Ibid., 84. Emphasis added.
5   We also note that Marcel's decision to write his novel occurs in the final volume of *In Search of Lost Time* and that the novel we have just finished is that novel he intends to begin. Since the novel is written in retrospect, it is a product of Marcel's reflection or of what Voegelin in his late work designated "reflective distance." Cf. Eric Voegelin, *Order and History, Volume V: In Search of Order,* vol. 18 of *The Collected Works of Eric Voegelin*, ed. Ellis Sandoz (Columbia, MO: University of Missouri Press, 2000), 54–56.

I was undecided as to my title. Should I use the definite article *the* as in "*In Search of Lost Time*: *The* Biography of Consciousness," or should I use the indefinite article *a* as in "*In Search of Lost Time*: *A* Biography of Consciousness"? So, I have entitled my reflections on Proust "*In Search of Lost Time*: Biographies of Consciousness" in order to avail myself of the advantages of both the definite and the indefinite articles. There must, however, be some clarification of this decision. Marcel/Proust provides us the clue in two passages in the final volume, *Time Regained*. He writes that "this life that we live in half-darkness can be illumined, this life that at every moment we distort can be restored to its true pristine shape, that a *life, in short, can be realised within the confines of a book*!"[6] Marcel experiences an avalanche of "*diverses impressions bienheureuses*"[7] that resuscitate the timeless being within him.[8] With the resuscitation of the timeless being within him, he discovers his vocation to write the book he has long intended to write, and this book will be the biography of his life, both of the being who is subject to time and the timeless being within.

Moreover, Marcel gives us an idea of how he understands the nature of the book that he will now begin. The following passage hints that his novel is "the" biography of Marcel's consciousness,

6   Proust, *Time Regained*, VI: 507. Emphasis added.
7   "Impressions" is the term that Marcel uses in *Time Regained*, the last volume of *In Search of Lost Time*, to name these specific events of his consciousness. See *Le temps retrouvé, À la recherché du temps perdu* (Gallimard, 1999), where Proust uses the term "*diverses impressions bienheureuses*" (2266). In *In Search of Lost Time* (Proust, *Time Regained*, VI: 262), this phrase is translated as "diverse happy impressions." I prefer the more metaphysical or spiritual translation of "various blessed impressions," for these impressions are more than just happy. This translation, I think, is closer to both the nature of the experiences themselves and to the spirit of Proust's meditation in the final volume. These events may be understood to be experiences defined as "transactions within consciousness." Cf. Ellis Sandoz, Introduction to Eric Voegelin, *Published Essays, 1966–1985*, vol. 12 of *The Collected Works of Eric Voegelin*, ed. Ellis Sandoz (Columbia, MO: University of Missouri Press, 1990), xx. In the earlier volumes Marcel describes these events using various terms.
8   Proust, *Time Regained*, VI: 332.

but it may also be "a" biography of his reader—and perhaps of Everyman.

> . . . I thought more modestly of my book and it would be inaccurate even to say that I thought of those who would read it as "my" readers. For it seemed to me that they would not be "my" readers but the readers of their own selves, my book being merely a sort of magnifying glass like those which the optician at Combray used to offer his customers—it would be my book, but with its help I would furnish them with the means of reading what lay inside themselves. So that I should not ask them to praise me or to censure me, but simply to tell me whether "it really is like that," I should ask them whether the words that they read within themselves are the same as those which I have written (though a discrepancy in this respect need not always be the consequence of an error on my part, since the explanation could also be that the reader had eyes for which my book was not a suitable instrument).[9]

The Biography of Consciousness

In order to sketch Marcel's biography of consciousness I will focus on three significant events in his life. The first—which points up the importance of habit and its barriers against uncertainty and melancholy—occurs during his childhood at Combray. The second event—the madeleine episode as the first manifestation of a developed "blessed impression"—occurs in Paris during his early manhood.[10] The third "event" occurs at the home of the Prince and Princesse de Guermantes and consists of an avalanche of the various "diverse blessed impressions" that have been visited upon him throughout his life.

9   Ibid., 508.
10   We cannot know exactly when this occurred but it seems to have occurred around the time that Marcel longed to be accepted into society of Parisian salons, especially the Duke and Duchess de Guermantes.

Marcel's bedroom in Combray:
the stirrings of childhood consciousness

Marcel's initial reflection on Habit is prefaced by his opening reflections on sleeping, dreaming, and waking in the first pages of the first volume of the novel, *Swann's Way*—the novel that he has resolved to write at the close of the seventh and final volume, *Time Regained*. Looking back upon his life, Marcel remembers the various bedrooms in which he has slept and the need for him to habituate himself to the contents of those bedrooms. Before he remembers his bedroom as a child, however, he reflects upon his (and Everyman's) place in the cosmos as he sleeps.

His meditation on sleeping, dreaming, and waking enables him to place himself in a spatio-temporal cosmos while at the same time permitting him to recognize that not only does the body transcend into the world of space, but that his consciousness itself as it awakens from sleep recapitulates the historical development of human consciousness from the "the most rudimentary sense of existence, such as may lurk and flicker in the depths of an animal's consciousness," through a cave-dweller's experience, and into his contemporary time. Marcel writes: "When a man is asleep, he has in a circle round him the chain of the hours, the sequence of the years, the order of the heavenly bodies. Instinctively he consults them when he awakes, and in an instant reads off his own position on the earth's surface and the time that has elapsed during his slumbers; but this ordered procession is apt to grow confused, and to break its ranks."[11] It is against this backdrop that he remembers

11 Proust, *Swann's Way*. I: 4. Compare this passage with Eric Voegelin's statement in "The Beginning and the Beyond," where he writes: "I shall begin . . . from the cosmos as it impresses itself on man by the splendor of its existence, by the movements of the starry heavens, by the intelligibility of its order, and by its lasting as the habitat of man. The man who receives the impression, in his turn, is endowed with *an intellect both questioning and imaginative*. . . . In this experience of the cosmos, *neither the impression nor the reception of reality is dully factual. It rather is alive with the meaning of a spiritual event*, for the impression is revelatory of the divine mystery, while the reception responds to the revelatory component by cognition of faith." Eric Voegelin, *What is History? and Other Late Unpublished Writings*, vol. 28 of *The Collected Works of Eric Voegelin*, ed. Thomas A.

the bedroom in which he slept at his grandparents' house in Combray. With this remembrance we are introduced to his reflections on Habit, "that skilful but slow-moving arranger who begins by letting our minds suffer for weeks on end in temporary quarters, but whom our minds are none the less only too happy to discover at last, for without it, reduced to their own devices, they would be powerless to make any room seem habitable."[12] When he awakens in the middle of the night, Habit has permitted him to recognize that he is in his own bedroom and, instead of returning to sleep, Marcel recalls his life in the old days, but especially Combray. As he remembers his childhood at Combray we are introduced to an overwhelmingly important event in the historical development of his consciousness.

> At Combray, as every afternoon ended, long before the time when I should have to go to bed and lie there, unsleeping, far from my mother and grandmother, my bedroom became the fixed point on which my melancholy and anxious thoughts were centred. Someone had indeed had the happy idea of giving me, to distract me on evenings when I seemed abnormally wretched, a magic lantern, which used to be set on top of my lamp while we waited for dinner-time to come; and, after the fashion of the master-builders and glass-painters of Gothic days, it substituted for the opaqueness of my walls an impalpable iridescence, supernatural phenomena of many colours, in which legends were depicted as on a shifting and transitory window. But my sorrows were only increased thereby, because this mere change of lighting was enough to destroy the familiar impression I had of my room, thanks to which, save for the torture of going to bed, it had become quite endurable.[13]

Hollweck and Paul Caringella (Baton Rouge, LA: Louisiana State University Press, 1990), 177 (emphasis added).
12 Ibid., 8–9.
13 Ibid., 9–10.

While being charmed by these "bright projections, which seemed to emanate from a Merovingian past and shed around me the reflections of such ancient history," Marcel was nevertheless distressed by them. He writes: "But I cannot express the discomfort I felt at this intrusion of mystery and beauty into a room which I had succeeded in filling with my own personality until I thought no more of it than of myself. The anaesthetic effect of habit being destroyed, I would begin to think—and to feel—such melancholy things."[14] This is the first hint of Marcel's anxiety, an anxiety that he associates with his fear of death and that he explicitly recognizes when in the final volume he writes: "this [the impressions that exist outside time] explained why it was that my anxiety on the subject of my death had ceased at the moment when I had unconsciously recognized the taste of the little madeleine, since the being which at that moment I had been was an extra-temporal being and therefore unalarmed by the vicissitudes of the future."[15]

The disturbance induced in him by the magic lantern is not the only instance of his childhood anxiety, however, for each night Marcel is reluctant to go to bed unless his Mamma kisses him goodnight. Even after her kiss he keeps calling her back for one more kiss. On one particular night when he had to go to bed alone since Charles Swann was visiting, he attempted to persuade his mother to come to his bedroom by sending her a note. She refused, at which point he left his bedroom to sit on the stairs and await her coming up to bed. He feared that this would be disastrous for him because his strict father was accompanying her as she climbed the stairs. Much later, as recounted in *Time Regained*, he remembers this night, the night when his father gave in to his pleadings by permitting his mother not only to enter his bedroom but to sleep the night there also. Seeing a copy of George Sand's novel *François le Champi* in the Prince de Guermantes's library, Marcel recalls the fateful night in Combray,

> during the night that was perhaps the sweetest and saddest of
> my life, when I had alas! . . . won from my parents that first

14 Ibid., 11.
15 Proust, *Time Regained*, VI: 262.

abdication of their authority from which, later, I was to date the decline of my health and my will, and my renunciation, each day disastrously confirmed, of a task that daily became more difficult—and rediscovered by me today, in the library of these same Guermantes, on this most wonderful of all days which had suddenly illuminated for me not only the old groping movements of my thought, but even the whole purpose of my life and perhaps of art itself. [16]

After Marcel experiences the avalanche of "diverse blessed impressions," he longs for the strength that he had the night that his parents acceded to his wishes. "Ah!" he writes, "if only I now possessed the strength which had still been intact on that evening brought back to my mind by the sight of *François le Champi*!" [17]

From these bedroom episodes flow the continuance of Marcel's anxiety, ill health, and fear of death, and his attempts to forestall boredom and dreariness through a socializing that would supplant with diverting amusements his ambition to write.[18]

The *petite madeleine* episode:
the continuity of childhood in the consciousness of youth

Everyone knows (or at least has heard of) the episode of the *petite madeleine*, but for clarity I will summarize. Marcel is living in Paris with his parents. His mother, seeing that he is cold, offers him tea and, when he accepts, sends for some *petites madeleines*. Marcel is dispirited after a dreary day "with the prospect of a depressing morrow," and he takes a spoonful of the tea in which he had dipped a morsel of the madeleine. Then he remembers:

16   Ibid., 287.
17   Ibid., 525–26.
18   It should also be pointed out, however, that very often adults of his father's acquaintance would discourage the young Marcel from pursuing his writing, and that at least once Marcel misunderstood a compliment from the Bergotte, the writer.

No sooner had the warm liquid mixed with the crumbs touched my palate than a shiver ran through me and I stopped, intent upon the extraordinary thing that was happening to me. An exquisite pleasure had invaded my senses, something isolated, detached, with no suggestion of its origin. And at once the vicissitudes of life had become indifferent to me, its disasters innocuous, its brevity illusory—this new sensation having had the effect, which love has, of filling me with a precious essence; or rather this essence was not in me, it *was* me. I had ceased to feel mediocre, contingent, mortal. Whence could it have come to me, this all-powerful joy? I sensed that it was connected with the taste of the tea and the cake, but that it infinitely transcended those savours, could not, indeed, be of the same nature. Where did it come from? What did it mean? How could I seize and apprehend it?[19]

Marcel then attempts to recreate the sensation by repeating his taking of the tea with the madeleine—once, twice, but the sensation is not repeated. He cannot get to the bottom of what the experience means, and why this unremembered state brought indisputable evidence "of its felicity, its reality" with it, for it was accompanied by no logical proof. But suddenly "the memory revealed itself. The taste was that of the little piece of madeleine which on Sunday mornings at Combray . . . when I went to say good morning to her in her bedroom, my aunt Léonie used to give me, dipping it first in her own cup of tea or tisane."[20]

And as in the game wherein the Japanese amuse themselves by filling a porcelain bowl with water and steeping in it little pieces of paper which until then are without character or form, but, the moment they become wet, stretch and twist and take on colour and distinctive shape, become flowers or houses or people, solid and recognisable, in that moment all the flowers in our garden and in M. Swann's park, and the water-lilies on

19 Proust, *Swann's Way*, I: 60.
20 Ibid., 63.

the Vivonne and the good folk of the village and their little dwellings and the parish church and the whole of Combray and its surroundings, taking shape and solidity, sprang into being, town and gardens alike, from my cup of tea.[21]

After Marcel records another blessed impression—the appearance of the twin steeples of Martinville that appeared to him while riding beside the driver in Dr. Percepied's carriage[22]—he understands the signal importance that Combray and his experiences there play in his life. He reflects that the "Méséglise way" and "Guermantes way" from his childhood walks in Combray "remain linked with many of the little incidents of life" and from "the deepest layer of my mental soil, as the firm ground on which I will stand. . . . It is because I believed in things and in people . . . ."[23]

The avalanche of diverse blessed impressions: the fruit of age

After twenty years—some of which have been spent in a sanitarium—of not "going into society," Marcel accepts an invitation to attend a party at the mansion of the Prince and Princesse de Guermantes. It is at this party that an avalanche of impressions rushes down upon him. He remembers that Bergotte complimented him long ago by remarking that, despite his illness, he could not be pitied for he possessed "the joys of the mind." He despairs:

> [H]ow mistaken he had been about me! How little joy there
> was in this sterile lucidity! Even if sometimes perhaps I had
> pleasures (not of the mind), I sacrificed them always to one
> woman after another; so that, had fate granted me another
> hundred years of life and sound health as well, it would

21 Ibid., 64.
22 Ibid., 255–56.
23 Ibid., 258, 259–60. His belief in things and people—what he calls "the faith which creates"—had ceased to exist in him, until this faith is restored in the avalanche of "diverse blessed impressions" that he records in the final volume.

merely have added a series of extensions to an already tedious existence, which there seemed to be no point in prolonging at all, still less for any great length of time. As for the "joys of the intelligence," could I call by that name those cold observations which my clairvoyant eye or my power of accurate ratiocination made without any pleasure and which remained always infertile?[24]

Immediately, however, Marcel notes:

But it is sometimes just at the moment when we think that everything is lost that the intimation arrives which may save us; one has knocked at all the doors which lead nowhere, and then one stumbles without knowing it on the only door through which one can enter—which one might have sought in vain for a hundred years—and it opens of its own accord.[25]

Not only did he stumble on the only door available, but he literally stumbled on an uneven paving stone while entering the Prince's mansion that triggered the first of many resurrected impressions. Unexpectedly these uneven cobblestones return Marcel to St. Mark's in Venice and the feelings of great joy he had experienced there. Marcel notices.

Because a musical performance is in progress, he is shown into the Prince's library to await entrance to the party. In the library the avalanche of "visitations" continues, visitations that he calls "diverse blessed impressions."[26] They are all triggered by some objective stimulus—uneven

24 Proust, *Time Regained*, VI: 254.
25 Ibid., 254–55.
26 Although there are eleven accounts of these impressions throughout the novel—depending on who is counting—four receive expanded treatment at Marcel's hands. These include: the *petite madeleine* (*Swann's Way*, I: 60–64); church steeples at Martinville (*Swann's Way*, I: 252–57); "Intermittences of the heart," in which the impression resurrects Marcel's dead grandmother (*Sodom and Gomorrah*, IV: 210–19); and the "avalanche" before the Prince de Guermantes's mansion and in his library (*Time Regained*, VI: 255–332).

paving stones, the sound of water running through pipes, the stiffness of a napkin touched to his lips, the clink of a spoon on china, the sight of George Sand's novel *François le Champi* that he read as a child in Combray. All of the varied experiences throughout Marcel's life, experiences that are secreted into but unremarked in the chronicle of his activities from his adolescence into manhood until his retirement from society, are resurrected. This avalanche leads Marcel to ask himself: "why had the images of Combray and of Venice, at these two different moments, given me joy which was like a certainty and which sufficed, without any other proof, to make death a matter of indifference to me?"[27] This time, however, unlike his abandoned earlier attempts upon the appearance of an impression, Marcel resolves to understand the meaning of these resurrections of the past. What follows is a meditation on what these impressions communicate, for even though he realizes that these impressions have resurrected "the timeless man within me" and that this timeless being had always existed in him, he commits himself to penetrating to the meaning of these experiences.[28]

This meditation strikingly illustrates Voegelin's symbolization of the philosopher's consciousness of "his participatory role in the process of experience, imagination, and symbolization" as well as the "reflective distance of [his] consciousness to its own participation in thing-reality and It-reality."[29] Both a philosopher and a novelist must rely upon this capacity for reflective distance as they imaginatively create a narrative and recreate the meaning embedded in the events experienced during their lives. In the case of Marcel, this meditation occurs late in his life when he can look back on his life and remember those experiences in time that had happened to him but had not been lost. *In Search of Lost Time*, then, is one long meditation rooted in the capacity of the novelist, Marcel, to reflect upon the events of his life in time past—or in this case time lost. Additionally, *In Search of Lost Time* is one long meditation

27 Proust, *Time Regained*, VI: 257.
28 This meditation runs for about sixty pages. Ibid., 255–332.
29 Voegelin, *In Search of Order*, 54–55. The symbols "thing-reality and It-reality" were created by Voegelin in his late work to express his understanding of the nature of reality and the tension of human consciousness between the mortal and the immortal.

rooted in the imaginative capacity of the novelist, Proust, to reflect upon time lost and Time (the Timeless) regained.

Seeking to uncover why these blessed impressions had brought such happiness and certainty, Marcel reflects:

> The truth surely was that the being within me which had enjoyed these impressions had enjoyed them because . . . in some way they were extra-temporal and this being made its appearance only when . . . it was likely to find itself in the one and only medium in which it could exist and enjoy the essence of things, that is to say, outside time. This explained why it was that my anxiety on the subject of my death had ceased at the moment when I had unconsciously recognised the taste of the little madeleine, since the being which at that moment I had been was an extra-temporal being, and therefore unalarmed by the vicissitudes of the future.[30]

* * * * *

> The being which had been reborn in me . . . with a sudden shudder of happiness . . . is nourished only by the essences of things, in these alone does it find its sustenance and delight. In the observation of the present, where the senses cannot feed it with this food, it languishes, as it does in the consideration of a past made arid by the intellect or in the anticipation of a future which the will constructs with fragments of the present and the past . . . . But let a noise or a scent, once heard or once smelt, be heard or smelt again in the present and at the same time in the past, real without being actual, ideal without being abstract, and immediately the permanent and habitually concealed essence of things is liberated and our true self, which seemed—had perhaps for long years seemed—to be dead but was not altogether dead, is awakened

30 Proust, *Time Regained*, VI: 262.

and reanimated as it receives the celestial nourishment that is brought to it.[31]

After Marcel has begun to understand the impressions, he resolves to write his book. But now he must be concerned with the question of time, for he has resolved to make visible in a book realities that were outside Time.

In summary we notice certain characteristics of Marcel's biography of consciousness. Foremost, we notice that Marcel's consciousness is formed historically and even though in its essence it is *timeless*, this timelessness is, from time to time, expressed *in time*, for after the avalanche of remembrances he realizes that he had been experiencing these visitations since his childhood. Moreover, he realizes at the Prince's party that "such impressions had been rather rare in my life, but they dominated it, and I could still rediscover in the past some of these peaks which I had unwisely lost sight of (a mistake I would be careful not to make again)."[32]

From childhood, however, Marcel's life is fraught with anxiety, ill health, and the fear of death. These fears and anxieties lead him to seek solace in feverish social activity to combat the dreariness of his days and even attempts to halt the "delicate vacillations of reality,"[33] especially, for example, through his efforts to control and dictate his lover Albertine's every action.[34]

Many, if not most, of the diverse blessed impressions generate in Marcel feelings of great joy, feelings that, because they are experienced by his timeless being, bring in their wake no concern for his future, and that thereby overcome his fear of death.

Finally, once the timeless being within him is resurrected or resuscitated, Marcel accepts his vocation to write his book, the novel that the reader has almost finished reading at this point. Once again, Marcel is concerned with death but, unlike the earlier note of fear, his concern

---

31 Ibid., 264.
32 Ibid., 334.
33 Cf. Heimito von Doderer, *The Demons*, trs. Richard and Clara Winston (New York: Alfred A. Knopf, 1961), 1237.
34 Cf. Proust, *The Captive*, V: passim.

with death now rings in a new key—the hope that he will be granted enough time to finish his book.

> And I had to ask myself not only: "Is there still time?" but also: "Am I well enough?" Ill health, which by compelling me, like a severe director of conscience, to die to the world, had rendered me good service (for "except a corn of wheat fall into the ground and die, it abideth alone: but if it die, it bringeth forth much fruit"), and which, after idleness had preserved me from the dangers of facility, was perhaps going to protect me from idleness, that same ill health had consumed my strength and as I had first noticed long ago, particularly when I had ceased to love Albertine, the strength of my memory. But was not the re-creation by the memory of impressions which had then to be deepened, illumined, transformed into equivalents of understanding, was not this process one of the conditions, almost the very essence of the work of art as I had just now in the library conceived it? Ah! if only I now possessed the strength which had still been intact on that evening brought back to my mind by the sight of *François le Champi*![35]

He now realizes that a writer must have the

> strength to force himself to make an impression pass through all the successive states which will culminate in its fixation, its expression. The reality that he has to express resides, as I now began to understand, not in the superficial appearance of his subject but at a depth at which that appearance matters little; this truth had been symbolized for me by that clink of a spoon against a plate, that starched stiffness of a napkin, which had been of more value to me for my spiritual renewal than innumerable conversations of a humanitarian or patriotic or internationalist or metaphysical kind.[36]

35 Proust, *Time Regained*, VI: 525–26.
36 Ibid., 279.

Proust's understanding of the task of the novelist—as expressed in the reflections of Marcel—mirror Voegelin's understanding of how literature plays a crucial role in not only constituting our understanding of reality but in constituting reality itself. In a letter to his friend and literary critic, Robert B. Heilman, Voegelin responded to Heilman's surmise that particular literary works "constitute" reality by commenting on the creative and evocative power of literature. He wrote:

> I quite agree with you that literature constitutes reality, if it is any good, and does not merely imitate or interpret it. The starting point for theoretical consideration would be for me the Aristotelian observation (in the *Poetics*) that the poets give better insights into human nature than the historians, because they do not report reality but imaginatively create the "nature" of things. "Reality" as observed is always nature in the state of potentiality; the "true" reality of actualized nature is rarely a given, but must be constructed from the resources of the artist. In this Aristotelian conception the artist is forced to create, because the difference between the potentiality empirically given and actualization is absent from empirical reality. Unless the artist supplies the fullness of human nature as the background, the empirical reality will be as flat as it usually is.[37]

Once Proust creates the reality of *the* biography of Marcel's consciousness, that symbolization becomes the model for his readers to penetrate and thus create the reality of their own biographies.

A Biography of Consciousness?

Unfortunately, *a* biography of consciousness cannot be reduced to a set of demonstrable, universal characteristics derived from the pages of Proust. Nevertheless *In Search of Lost Time* may still be read as *a* biography of consciousness—that of Proust and that of a future reader.

---

37   Letter 91 in Embry, *A Friendship in Letters,* 210.

Because Proust wrote *In Search of Lost Time* as a novel—following Marcel's insight that a "life, in short, can be realised within the confines of a book"—I will take the liberty of calling it *a* biography of consciousness in a two-fold sense. It is both *the* biography of Marcel's consciousness, and *a* biography of consciousness, Proust's and *a* future reader's. By writing a novel and giving the narrator his own given name, Proust records both *the* biography of Marcel's consciousness and *a* biography of his own. That the latter is possible depends upon the imaginative-meditative capacity of the novelist Marcel/Proust— Marcel is the narrator-novelist and protagonist of *In Search of Lost Time*, a novel written, of course, by Marcel Proust. It is not without significance that Proust gives the narrator his Christian name and that any work of fiction is a product of the novelist's imagination. But *imagination* here is used in the sense that Marcel explains it in *Time Regained*, where he observes:

> So often, in the course of my *life*, *reality* had disappointed me because at the instant when my senses perceived it my *imagination*, which was the only *organ* that I possessed for the *enjoyment* of beauty, could not apply itself to it, in virtue of that ineluctable law which ordains that *we can only imagine what is absent*. And now, suddenly, the effect of this harsh law had been neutralized, temporarily annulled, by a marvelous expedient of nature which had caused a sensation . . . to be mirrored at one and the same time in the past, so that my *imagination* was permitted to savour it, and in the present, where the actual shock to my senses of the noise, the touch of the linen napkin, or whatever it might be, had added to the *dreams of the imagination* the concept of '*existence*' which they usually lack, and through this subterfuge had made it possible for my being to secure, to isolate, to immobilise— for a moment brief as a flash of lightning—what normally it never apprehends: a fragment of time in the pure state.[38]

38   Proust, *Time Regained*, VI: 263–64 (emphases added).

Imagination, however, includes more than just the capacity of a human being to conjure up circumstances and actions; it is a component both in the structure of reality and in the human consciousness that participates in that reality. For Eric Voegelin, human beings participate in reality as composite beings who are conscious of their participation as experiences. In 1952 he writes: "Science [philosophy] starts from the prescientific existence of man, from his participation in the world with his body, soul, intellect, and spirit, from his primary grip on all the realms of being that is assured to him because his own nature is their epitome."[39] And since human beings consciously experience their participation in reality, they are compelled to express this participatory experience in language. Marcel notes that imagination is the "organ" that enables him to experience and appreciate "beauty"; while Voegelin, in his late work, *In Search of Order*, explains that "imagination" denotes man's "ability to find the way from the metaleptic [participatory] experiences to the imagery of expressive symbols."[40] Furthermore, Voegelin writes: "There is no truth symbolized without man's imaginative power to find the symbols that will express his response to the appeal of reality; but there is no truth to be symbolized without the comprehending It-reality in which such structures as man with his participatory consciousness, experiences of appeal and response, language, and imagination occur."[41]

It is not unreasonable to assume, I think, that the novelist Marcel Proust has undergone the irrupting experiences of his own "timeless being within" that Marcel undergoes in the novel,[42] for if a reader of *In Search of Lost Time* engages the novel fully in a participatory reading

39 Eric Voegelin, *Modernity Without Restraint: The Political Religions; The New Science of Politics;* and *Science, Politics, and Gnosticism,* vol. 5 of *The Collected Works of Eric Voegelin,* ed. with Introduction by Manfred Henningsen (Columbia, MO: University of Missouri Press, 2000), 91.
40 Voegelin, *In Search of Order,* 52.
41 Ibid.
42 The truth of this assumption could only be demonstrated by an extensive discussion of Imagination and the Imaginative structure of reality as developed in the last work of Eric Voegelin, *In Search of Order.* Such an analysis, however, is beyond the scope of the present study.

[see below], he will be persuaded that Proust speaks to Everyman's experience. Proust himself must have undergone experiences that, like Voegelin, "excited [his] consciousness to the 'awe' of existence."[43] The advantage that an imaginative work of art affords the novelist Proust is that experiences or events of his consciousness may be appropriately symbolized in the story of Marcel's life. Proust does not have to reach old age or even die for his biography of consciousness to be written, for he can imaginatively meditate his own life and future death—for "except a corn of wheat fall into the ground and die, it abideth alone: but if it die, it bringeth forth much fruit"[44] —thereby making his "life transparent for death."[45]

The truth of the assertion that *In Search of Lost Time* is *a* future reader's biography of consciousness, depends upon the participation of this reader in Marcel's biography. This reader must then rely upon memory and comparison[46] in order to identify his or her individual (but equivalent) experiences that recall the events of the "timeless being within" experienced by Marcel throughout his life.

43 My not-so-hidden assumption here is that Proust could not have written *this* novel without having himself undergone "irrupting experiences and . . . the excitation they induce." Voegelin, *Anamnesis*, 84.

44 Proust, *Time Regained*, VI: 525.

45 This phrase is Voegelin's in a letter to Robert Heilman. Writing about the superiority of the poet over the historian he points out that "in this Aristotelian conception the artist is forced to create, because the difference between the potentiality empirically given and actualization is absent from empirical reality. Unless the artist supplies the fullness of human nature as the background, the empirical reality will be as flat as it usually is. As an example, take our pet grievance, the ideologist. If you simply describe him, he will be an unintelligible caricature; if you interpret him by a psychology of motivations, you will at best get the rationale of his actions. In order to bring him to life you will have to reflect on the problem of a man who wants to transform the world in his image. If you try that, you may find that there are men who cannot grow with themselves and cannot make their own life transparent for death." Embry, *A Friendship in Letters*, 210.

46 Eric Voegelin writes in the draft of an unsent letter to Karl E. Ettinger that "'Memory and comparison' are still the methods of the social sciences as they were when Aristotle laid down the rule." Embry, *A Friendship in Letters*, Appendix I.d, 316.

Marcel's life that is "realised within the confines of a book" doubles as *a* biography of consciousness, for Marcel asks his readers "simply to tell . . . [him] whether 'it really is like that,' I should ask them whether the words that they read within themselves are the same as those which I have written."[47] Proust's insights apply to Everyman in the same way that the insights of a philosopher are intended to invite Everyman to explore the nature of reality and the role that man plays in the community of being. Even though Marcel qualifies this request of his readers with a parenthetical insertion at the end of the sentence—"though a discrepancy in this respect need not always be the consequence of an error on my part, since the explanation could also be that the reader had eyes for which my book was not a suitable instrument"[48]—a reader who penetrates to the heart of Proust's novel will, I think, affirm the truth of Marcel's insights into his own humanity, a common humanity that he shares with his readers.

The bases for this affirmation across the ages by readers of literary works lie in what Voegelin—arguing against historicism and relativism in his 1956 letter to Robert Heilman—called "circumstanced equality." He asserted: "All men are on the same level of circumstanced equality."[49] Although Voegelin does not specify the circumstances that are equally faced by all human beings in all times and places, it is easy enough to create, through consulting one's own common sense, a list that will be agreed to by everyone. Thus we arrive at the following:

> All human beings are born into existence in time, which is shared by "other" being things.
> All human beings who are born into existence in time will cease to exist in time.
> All human beings possess bodies.
> Bodies participate in the existent world.
> All human beings possess consciousness.
> The human body is the "location" of consciousness.

47 Proust, *Time Regained*, VI: 508.
48 Ibid.
49 Embry, *A Friendship in Letters*, 158.

To this list, must be added:

> Consciousness participates in the non-existent "ground of being."

This last circumstance, uncovered and "remembered" in Voegelin's historical and personal search for order—the entirety of which explored and reflected upon the millennial "dialogue among men about their nature and destiny"—can also be verified by anyone who, avoiding preconceptions, is open to the exploration of his or her own consciousness.

Given the circumstanced equality between ourselves and Proust, how are we then to proceed in order to affirm the truth of *In Search of Lost Time*? A preliminary list of conditions includes—after the initial decision to read such a physically forbidding novel of over 4000 pages—first the necessary time and leisure. In some ways this first condition is equivalent to the condition required of anyone who reads philosophy or who philosophizes. Just as Proust needed time—years—to write the work and wealth enough to provide that time, we need the time to read the novel.

A reader must then prepare himself existentially to be "persuaded" or "moved" by fiction, in general, and by Proust's novel, in particular. I am reminded of the question that Polemarchos puts to Socrates near the beginning of Plato's *Republic* after Socrates avers that he could return to Athens if he could persuade Polemarchos and his friends to let him leave the Piraeus. Polemarchos asks: Could you persuade us if we refused to listen? Polemarchos knew that to be persuaded the hearer must first "adopt" an openness that includes a readiness to experience persuasion itself as an existential movement in the metaxy of his own existence. In our times, this existential openness includes not only the "willingness to be moved by a novel," but also a willingness to be reminded that a non-existent, timeless, reality lies behind the visible reality of our daily world. Flannery O'Connor believed that "good fiction" can only be understood by "the kind of mind that is willing to have its sense of mystery deepened by contact with reality, and its sense of reality deepened by contact with mystery."[50] Essentially, a novel can evoke and

50 Flannery O'Connor, "The Nature and Aim of Fiction," in *Mystery and*

transform the reader only if the reader relaxes his natural skepticism about fiction and its popularly perceived unreal nowhereness and prepares a space mid-way between belief and skepticism; the reader simply must open himself to letting the symbolization work its charm upon his body, intellect, imagination, soul, and spirit.

Third, once we have decided to read *In Search of Lost Time*, we must commit ourselves to actually enduring the burden of it until its long-anticipated end, for this novel confronts the reader "with problems and perplexities," as Hannah Arendt writes (about twentieth-century novels in general), "in which the reader must be prepared to engage himself if he is to understand it at all."[51] The engagement with the novel that Arendt emphasizes demands of its readers commitment to read and re-read passages, to reflect on these passages and ultimately to engage in what I have elsewhere called a "participatory reading."[52] Such a "participatory reading" depends upon the conscious participation of the human being in reality and in the symbolic constellation of the novel, but above all it aims at an imaginative reenactment. Athanasios Moulakis in his Introduction to Voegelin's *World of the Polis* asserts that Voegelin "invites his reader to a *pia interpretatio* of the decisive documents, which does not mean the recognition of external authority or verities to be accepted on faith, but an inner preparation, a participatory disposition of the interpreter."[53] Ellis Sandoz also stressed participation by the reader of literature in the epilogue to the second edition of his study of Dostoevsky's

Manners: Occasional Prose (New York: Farrar, Straus & Giroux, 1961), 79.

51 Hannah Arendt, "Introduction" to Hermann Broch, *The Sleepwalkers*, trs. Willa and Edwin Muir (New York: The Universal Library, Grosset & Dunlap, 1947, 1949), v.

52 The remainder of this essay has been adapted from Embry, *The Philosopher and The Storyteller*, 57–60. The notion of participatory reading is grounded in my reading and teaching over many years not only of Voegelin's work, but also of literature. It was formulated in the context of creating an understanding of Voegelin's philosophy in its relation to literature.

53 Athanasios Moulakis, Editor's Introduction to Eric Voegelin, *Order and History, Volume II: The World of the Polis*, ed. Athanasios Moulakis, vol. 15 of *The Collected Works of Eric Voegelin* (Columbia: University of Missouri Press, 2000), 24. Hereinafter cited as Voegelin, *World of the Polis*.

"Legend of the Grand Inquisitor." He writes that "the readers enter into the work itself as participants, and they do not emerge from it the same as they were before."[54] "Participation," of course, plays a central role in the work of Voegelin. Hence the reader must be prepared to participate in the novel—as in a work of philosophy—and this participation requires the full engagement of the reader's nature as a human being—body, soul, intellect, imagination, and spirit—while relying upon the intentional and luminous dimensions of consciousness and exercising the cognitive-imaginative faculties of consciousness.

Athanasios Moulakis also observed that in Voegelin's mode of reading Plato, his "purpose was not to cull precepts from the past, but to reenact, at an advanced level of differentiation, Plato's response to the crisis of Athens. Reenactment meant taking to heart an exemplary lesson, which can only be properly understood by being reenacted, i.e., by reconstructing the motivating experiences behind the verbal and symbolic forms that have come down to us as documentary evidence."[55] An open existence is at once the precondition for this reenactment and the consequence of the evocative nature of the novel that results in reenactment.

Existence in openness is complex, paradoxical, and mysterious, much like the philosophical search itself is mysterious. It is as though one were to command the reader: "Be open to what the novel has to teach you about yourself and the world in which you live," when in fact the only way to persuade the reader of the need for openness is to provide a reason for being open. Viktor Frankl observed that if you want a person to laugh you cannot command him to laugh, you must tell him a joke.[56] The novel in our discussion is analogous to the joke in Frankl's observation. So, while at one level evocation must begin with the reader's predisposition to openness before encountering the symbols in the novel, at another level the encounter with the novel's symbols is what must open the reader to its truth. Readers, like the interlocutors in Plato's dialogues,

54 Ellis Sandoz, *Political Apocalypse: A Study of Dostoevsky's Grand Inquisitor*, second edition (Wilmington, Delaware: ISI Books, 2000), 276.
55 Moulakis, Editor's Introduction to Voegelin, *World of the Polis*, 3.
56 Viktor Frankl, *Man's Search for Meaning*, translated by Ilse Lasch, Foreword by Harold S. Kushner, Afterword by William J. Winslade (Boston: Beacon Press, 1959, 2003), 138.

must be moved to remember the mortal-immortal nature of their own existence as human beings. A novel that is any good will stimulate this memory. If the reader permits the novel to work its magic, he will be reminded of the composite nature of his humanity and thereby invited into the loving search for the truth of his existence.

Finally, a reader who confronts a difficult and complex novel must imaginatively and meditatively submerge himself in the story, for it is ultimately the reader's meditation rooted in the human capacity for reflective distance that enables him to make sense of or to discover the sense and meaning of the novel. While it is not possible to describe how this meditative submersion occurs, it is only through this process that the reader participates in the novel as a symbolization that has mysteriously emerged from the existential movement in the metaxy of the novelist.

Conclusion

As participatory readers of *In Search of Lost Time*, we are reminded that our consciousness is historically formed, that the experiences of the timeless from childhood through youth into middle and old age occur to us if we but notice and do not cut ourselves off from that Time "in the pure state" or, as Plato would phrase it, from time as the *eikon* of eternity. We may also come to understand that our experiences of the timeless, while individual, are unique only in their specific and temporally bound details, and that these details share with other human beings a deep structure of meaning rooted in the timeless structure of reality. We are reminded by Marcel that his "blessed impressions" are equivalent in essence to those of other writers such as those recorded by Chateaubriand in his own *Memoirs*. Proust asks his readers:

> Is it not from a sensation of the same species as that of the madeleine that Chateaubriand suspends the loveliest episode in the *Mémoires d'Outre-tombe*: "Yesterday evening I was walking alone . . . I was roused from my reflections by the warbling of a thrush perched upon the highest branch of a birch tree. Instantaneously the magic sound caused my

father's estate to reappear before my eyes; I forgot the catastrophes of which I had recently been the witness and, transported suddenly into the past, I saw again those country scenes in which I had so often heard the fluting notes of the thrush."[57]

Marcel also recalls other instances similar in nature to that of his experience of the madeleine. "And in one of the masterpieces of French literature, Gérard de Nerval's *Sylvie* . . . there figures a sensation of the same species as the taste of the Madeleine and the warbling of the thrush. Above all in Baudelaire, where they are more numerous still, reminiscences of this kind are clearly less fortuitous and therefore, to my mind, unmistakable in their significance."[58]

Like Marcel, Proust's readers are proffered the opportunity to meditate upon their own biographies of consciousness, for it is this imaginative meditation that enables us to make sense, to *discover* the sense and meaning, of our lives. *In Search of Lost Time* may evoke in us—by reminding us of our own blessed impressions—the joy and unconcern for the future that flow from Marcel's diverse blessed impressions. It may, indeed, remind us that it is only from the experiences of our own blessed impressions that we may make our lives "transparent for our death."

57   Proust, *Time Regained*, VI: 334–35.
58   Ibid., 335.

Proust, Transcendence, and Metaxic Existence
Glenn Hughes

In his essay "Eternal Being in Time" (1964), the philosopher Eric Voegelin wrote that to be human means to "remain in the 'in-between,' in a temporal flow of experience in which eternity is nevertheless present," and that at every moment in the human flow of existence "there persists the tension toward eternal being transcending time."[1] In Voegelin's philosophical anthropology, the central fact he always returns to—because it is so easily forgotten in the modern climate of opinion—is that human existence is an "in-between" of immanence and transcendence, of participation in both temporal and timeless meaning. Throughout his later work, his favored term for referring to this "in-between" is the Greek word *metaxy*—a word he borrowed from Plato's dialogues, and turned into a *terminus technicus* for his analysis of personal, social, and historical existence.

Marcel Proust, in his seven-volume novel *In Search of Lost Time*, likewise presents human life as existence in the metaxy—that is, as existence permanently "in tension toward eternal being." In this essay I explore Proust's literary vision of metaxic existence, first in order to discover in what significant ways it corresponds to Voegelin's philosophical analysis of human existence as life in the metaxy. Then I will indicate some of the ways in which the metaxic vision of Proust differs from that of Voegelin, using some elements of Voegelin's analysis to engage in a brief critique of certain features of Proust's view of human

1   Eric Voegelin, "Eternal Being in Time," in Voegelin, *Anamnesis: On the Theory of History and Politics*, vol. 6 of *The Collected Works of Eric Voegelin*, trans. M. J. Hanak based upon the abbreviated version originally translated by Gerhart Niemeyer, ed. with Introduction by David Walsh (Columbia, MO: University of Missouri Press, 2002), 329.

participation in timeless reality. This critique will be quite narrow in scope, however, as it will not extend to other philosophical components of Proust's portrayal of the human condition that invite critical attention, such as his presentations of intersubjectivity; love; moral obligation; the epistemological relationship between subject and object; and so on. Such philosophical themes will be touched upon in the course of the essay, but only as needed to produce a proper account and accurate critique of Proust's vision of existence as an "in-between" of immanence and transcendence.

The *Search* is a novel, of course, not a philosophical treatise. Thus as a literary artist Proust's principal obligation is to *show*—not to explicate in a systematic, explanatory way—the truths he wishes to convey about human nature, basic experiences of consciousness, the self's relation to world, society, time and eternity, and other matters of elementary existential concern. At the same time, this *showing* in Proust's work often takes the form of portraying how a person—specifically the "I" of the novel—may reflect upon such truths and explain them at great length. How far are we justified, one might ask, in taking these expressed thoughts—in particular as pertaining to the vision of human life as existence in the metaxy—as representing Proust's own view of the human situation?

In order to approach an answer to this question, we need to distinguish three authorial "voices" in the novel. The first voice we may call that of the Narrator. Structurally, the entire novel is the narration, in the first person singular, of one character recounting his childhood, development, and most important his formative experiences. The second voice belongs to the Narrator's younger and growing self, starting with childhood memories, and reflects feelings, thoughts, and perceptions from within the horizon, or viewpoint, of that self at some stage in his development—a self referred to by the name "Marcel" at two points in the novel. At the very end of the novel's 4,300 pages, "Marcel's" voice converges and becomes one with the voice of the Narrator—as the Narrator/Marcel, having discovered his vocation, prepares to begin writing the novel we have just read. Finally, there is a third voice in the novel, the voice of Proust the author, which can to a degree be isolated from both that of Marcel and the Narrator, since a good deal of what Marcel says and does and what the Narrator writes about his own life does not correspond with important facts and details in Proust's biography.

But is it really legitimate to distinguish this third voice within the novel itself? There are compelling reasons for affirming that it is. The most important of these is that it is possible to find in Proust's many letters (and in his essays) the sincere, often impassioned, expression of judgments and viewpoints that are exactly reproduced in comments made by Marcel or by the Narrator in the novel.[2] Reading the novel, one finds certain assertions and assessments about consciousness, the self, society, and the human situation to be carefully repeated and consistently elaborated on; and when these same assertions can be found in writings where Proust speaks for himself, it is reasonable to conclude that they represent Proust's own considered judgments. And this is the case for all important passages pertaining to the affirmation of human participation in a reality beyond time and space, that is, to the vision of human existence as metaxic.

Still, why emphasize this distinction between the Narrator's (or Marcel's) voice, and Proust the writer's voice? Because there is some significance, it seems to me, in removing the novel's vision of human existence in the metaxy from the "what if" status of the point of view of a fictional Narrator. It is useful, from a philosophical point of view, to understand the novel's metaxic anthropology as Proust's own, because Proust—for all his oversights, biases, temperamental peculiarities, and even existential morbidities—was one of the twentieth century's most profound analysts of consciousness; and thus it is of philosophical value to be able to rely on the novel's presentation of the metaxy as Proust's own

---

2   "[I]ndisputably, there is the author himself who occasionally intervenes with his 'I' and makes generalizations and deductions. . . . [Often] the manner and matter of the comment make it clear that Proust is not merely speaking for Marcel [or the Narrator] but for himself. . . . [I]n his correspondence [Proust] often claims as his own the opinions expressed in the novel—opinions on art, on love, on friendship, on involuntary memory and the living past, on the lessons of experience in general; so that it is quite safe to assume that the *generalizations* of the novel are those of the author." Harold March, *The Two Worlds of Marcel Proust* (New York: A. S. Barnes & Company, Inc., Perpetua Edition, 1961), 171 (emphasis added)..

testimony, based on his own mystical experiences and careful self-re-flection, testimony that can be confidently relied upon in the effort to explain certain ontological and anthropological facts that must be em-braced if one is to live, as Voegelin would say, in the "truth of existence."

But if the affirmation of life as metaxic is central to Proust's own vi-sion of existence, it is also of utmost importance, artistically, to the unity and integrity of the novel. The novel is the story of a life, which, like all existence, is lived and suffered in time; and it soon becomes clear that *time as lived* is the theme of the novel. But time lived, Proust shows and tells us, can be seen to have an integral ontological form, and to constitute a genuine *story* rather than being just an aggregate of disconnected chronological episodes that are perishable, contingent, and finally mean-ingless, because of the fact that existence at all times is lived in the inter-section of time and eternity. And so just as human participation in eternal meaning and value is what gives any human life a unified form and struc-ture, so the written story of "Marcel's" life, as created and presented by Proust, gains its distinctive novelistic unity and form from the author's metaxic vision that, finally, illuminates and integrates all of its episodes.

This is why it is to the point to emphasize that Proust's novel—in its vastly digressive way, and amid many other objectives—most fundamen-tally tells the story of Marcel's ongoing intimations, and eventual explicit discovery, of the truth that human existence participates in eternal being "outside of time." However, because this discovery does not take place—and thus the unified meaningfulness of the life and the formal integrity of the novel are not revealed—until the final volume, *Time Regained*, the reader is left in the dark for a very long time about how the novel and the life whose story it tells "makes sense" as a whole. Given that the novel's seven volumes were published over the course of fourteen years (1913–1927), up until the time the final volume appeared (five years after Proust's death), the whole work appeared to many readers and critics to be formless and disconnected—not to mention endless. As Roger Shat-tuck points out, "[i]t looked at first like a conspiracy against readers."[3] But the concluding volume's clear and extensively elaborated account of

3   Roger Shattuck, *Proust's Way: A Field Guide to* In Search of Lost Time (New York: W. W. Norton & Company, 2000), 2.

the metaxic structure of Marcel's existence effectively radiates backwards over the whole work; elucidates many earlier passages that can now be recognized as hints of what is to come; reveals the necessity of all its elements; and shows that Proust carefully planned the novel's integrated form and—for all of his expansions, as he added and added to its original length during the years between the appearance of the various volumes—successfully kept the unity of this form under strict control through its grounding in his vision of human life as participation in eternal meaning.

Proust's Description of Existence in the Metaxy

To examine Proust's portrayal of life as existence in the in-between of time and eternity, I will first address Proust's affirmation of the following four points: 1) that there is a transcendent reality that humans participate in and can know of; 2) that humans experience transcendence only metaxically, that is, from within the interpenetration of time and timeless reality; 3) that for Proust, his existence in time is revealed to be a meaningful story *only* because it participates in eternal meaning; and 4) that there is no logical "proof," or need of any "proof," that the transcendent reality humans participate in "exists." To conclude this section, I will then discuss why Proust is properly described as a mystic, and then identify some of the existential paradoxes belonging to the structure of human self-understanding that Proust's mystical account of the human situation and search for meaning shows to be unavoidable and irresolvable.

To begin then: Proust is unequivocal, in the novel's final volume, *Time Regained*, in his assertion that there is a reality outside time, and that human beings can know of their participation in it. Marcel states that there is a "being within [him]" that is only able to undergo certain experiences because, in the course of having them, it consciously exists "outside time." In such moments, "freed from the order of time," "liberated from the contingencies of time," Marcel tastes the "contemplation . . . of eternity"; and thereby is revealed both "a portion of our mind more durable" than the temporal self, along with a reality "whose value [is] eternal."[4] The literary critic Harold March appropriately describes

4   Proust, *Time Regained*, VI: 262, 264–65, 268, 290, 301, 513.

these passages as constituting "a revelation of transcendent reality," and devotes a section of his book *The Two Worlds of Marcel Proust* to an analysis of Proust's account of "Transcendent Reality"[5]—a reality that Marcel describes wistfully, despite his joyful moments of participation in it, as continually "remote from our daily preoccupations," a reality "which it is very easy to die without having known" and yet which is "all the time immanent in [all] men . . . ."[6]

Second, Proust likewise makes it clear that transcendent reality is only experienced metaxically—that is, that the person who experiences it is not only immersed in time, but apprehends eternal reality only *through the medium of sensations and perceptions* that themselves belong intrinsically to the body embedded in the world of space and time.

This fact directs us to the novel's famous "epiphanies," the ecstatic moments of existing simultaneously both in and outside of time, which Proust in *Time Regained* calls at one point, in an inclusive reference, *impressions bienheureuses*—"happy impressions," or "felicitous impressions," or perhaps "blissful moments" or "privileged moments."[7] The most famous of these *impressions bienheureuses* is described early in the novel when Marcel, as an adult, tasting crumbs of a madeleine in a spoonful of tea, is suddenly immersed in intense and, to his consciousness, *present* realities of certain childhood experiences, experiences he relives with a completeness and fullness of perception and feeling—experiences in their "first, full effulgence"—that no effort of voluntary memory, or effort at intellectual recollection, could ever come close to

5   March, *The Two Worlds of Marcel Proust*, 216; see 216–28.
6   Proust, *Time Regained*, VI: 298.
7   Cf. Proust, *Time Regained*, VI: 262, where "*diverses impressions bien-heureuses*" is translated "diverse happy impressions." The meaning of the French term *impressions* as Proust uses it here is perhaps not best translated by the English word "impressions"; though a phrase such as "felicitous impressions" or (as used by Charles R. Embry in this volume) "blessed impressions" has the virtue of remaining close to Proust's language and meaning. I will rely on the French phrase *impressions bienheureuses* for the most part, but occasionally employ an English substitute such as "epiphanies."

evoking.[8] The novel describes, depending on just how one chooses to define them, somewhere between eleven and fifteen such *impressions bienheureuses*—not accounting for episodes where Marcel appears to turn away from, or somehow abort, such an experience.[9] Most critics agree that there are seven or eight such *impressions* that are crucial for understanding what Proust intends to convey through their descriptions. And that intention is this: that thr*ough the medium of certain sensory experiences*—although trivial enough in themselves—we can attain to glimpses of eternal reality and our participation in it; and, further, that the joy such moments almost always evoke in us, together with the certitude that our temporal lives involve participation in eternal reality, assures us that our lives have meaning and value. As a result of such *impressions bienheureuses*, we no longer need fear that our lives are nothing but pointless affairs of living, suffering, and aging in a reality that consists merely of perishable spatiotemporal duration.

As described in the novel, there are three sources of *impressions bienheureuses*. One is the *contemplation of nature* (including human-made structures); a second is *experiences of art* (literature, painting, and music

8   Edmund White, *Marcel Proust* (New York: Viking, 1999), 143. The episode appears in Proust, *Swann's Way*, I: 60–64.
9   Roger Shattuck, in his expert *Proust's Way*, identifies fifteen key *impressions bienheureuses* (or, as he calls them, *moments bienheureux*—although the latter phrase, as far as I can find, does not appear in Proust's novel), the last five of which (occurring in the grand series of "epiphanies" or "reminiscences" mid-way through *Time Regained*) he presents as a single "event" of linked experiences, giving him eleven such "events." In "Appendix II" of *Proust's Way* he offers a "Table of the *Moments Bienheureux*," with detailed analyses and elucidated patterns pertaining to each *moment*, along with an account of what is common to all of them; see Shattuck, *Proust's Way*, 257–64. Samuel Beckett, in his 1931 study *Proust*, after mentioning that these moments of "miracle" occur "twelve or thirteen times" in the novel, proceeds later to list and describe eleven of these "sacred actions." All of the events identified by Beckett are present in Shattuck's more complete "Table"; but Beckett, with one exception—that arising from Marcel's listening to Vinteuil's Septet in *La Prisonnière* (*The Captive*)—has identified all the major ones. See Samuel Beckett, *Proust; and Three Dialogues with Georges Duthuit* (London: John Calder, 1965), 34, 36–37.

are particularly important in Marcel's story, but architecture, theater, sculpture, and other arts play their parts); and the third—and by far the most important source—is *experiences of "involuntary memory,"* such as the experience provoked by Marcel's tasting of madeleine crumbs in spoonfuls of tea.

To treat the most important source first: in the episodes of involuntary memory, a sensory experience in the lived present brings flooding into Marcel's consciousness a similar, or analogous, sensory experience from his past life, but in a manner that is uncanny and deeply meaningful because the past sensation is not experienced as located in the past but as *present*. That is, the self suddenly becomes "the self that originally lived" the past sensation, while it yet remains the self living and experiencing the similar or analogous present sensation.[10] In this "magnetism of an identical moment," the self is not merely aware of, but *is*—this is Proust's central point—the self of both "times."[11] His explanation of how such a phenomenon can occur centers on two affirmations.

The first affirmation is this. A present sensation—for example, the first *impression* of the five linked epiphanies in *Time Regained*, which entails Marcel's experience of standing on "uneven paving-stones" in the courtyard of the Guermantes mansion in Paris—can, involuntarily and with an overwhelming vividness and thoroughness of remembrance, evoke a past sensation, in this case a *precisely similar* feeling of standing on "two uneven stones" in the baptistery of St. Mark's Cathedral in Venice, because the two sensations share a common, timeless "essence," and at this moment Marcel has suddenly and involuntarily gained access to this essence.[12] The second affirmation follows: the self can in truth apprehend and "enjoy the essence of things," essences that constitute the true and timeless reality "behind" what we experience through our bodies, because there is a dimension of the self that is itself "extra-temporal." These two affirmations are the result of Proust's reflections on his most singularly profound *impressions*, as recounted in *Time Regained*. In that volume, the *impressions bienheureuses* of involuntary memory lead

10 Proust, *Sodom and Gomorrah*, IV: 212.
11 Proust, *Swann's Way*, I: 62.
12 Proust, *Time Regained*, VI: 255–57, 259.

Marcel, through careful and prolonged reflection on their nature and meaning, to conclude that "real" personal life, which is our enduring, timeless self, and "real" truth, which consists of the timeless essences of meaning, may be discovered by us when, experiencing "a quality common to two sensations, we succeed in extracting their common essence and in reuniting them to each other, liberated from the contingencies of time . . . ." When this occurs, consciousness arises to an enraptured apprehension of timeless and essential reality through the "miracle" of the self's "escape from the present," which is an escape from being bound to the merely temporal dimension of change, decay, and death.[13]

However, contrary to what Samuel Beckett asserts in his 1931 essay on the novel, this escape described by Marcel does not constitute an "obliteration" of time—that is, it is not an experience whose result is that "Time is dead."[14] Time is very much alive in the *impressions bienheureuses* of involuntary memory, even as the self "escapes from time," because the events are based on *sensations experienced through the time-bound body*. The *impressions bienheureuses* are sensorily drenched, and therefore drenched in time. In other words, they are moments of being *simultaneously* in time and outside time, in which time is experienced— as Proust describes it in an earlier volume—in a strange "contradiction of survival and annihilation," as the simultaneous attention to the sensations of time present and the regaining of sensations of time past produce a "synthesis of [the] survival and annihilation" of time.[15] This is why Proust's account of human access to timelessness is a description and evocation of existence in the metaxy: only *in* time and *through* time, Proust's descriptions and explanations show, can timeless, eternal reality be humanly experienced. In the *impressions bienheureuses* of involuntary memory, consciousness experiences—in a phrase used by both T. S. Eliot and Voegelin—timelessness *intersecting* time.[16]

13 Ibid., 262–63, 290.
14 Beckett, *Proust*, 75.
15 Proust, *Sodom and Gomorrah*, IV: 215, 216.
16 See T. S. Eliot, *Four Quartets* (London: Faber and Faber, 1959), 44 ("The Dry Salvages," ll. 201–202); and Eric Voegelin, "Immortality: Experience and Symbol," in *Published Essays, 1966–1985*, ed. Ellis Sandoz, vol. 12 of *The Collected Works of Eric Voegelin* (Columbia MO: University of Mis-

This "in-between" vision of existence is underscored by Proust through his emphasis that in moments of involuntary memory, when the revelation of timeless reality occurs, the self becomes *intensely aware* of the particularity, the individual and unique existence, of the sensorily experienced objects of "time present." This runs counter to our everyday sensations and memories because, he explains, we habitually perceive and understand things only in terms of abstract and general concepts. But apprehension of the timeless essence of a thing produces in us a momentary lifting of this veil of habit and abstraction, bringing a sudden, illuminating recognition of the utter "originality," the pure "individual existence" of a thing, a place, or a person—what Duns Scotus and later Scholastics called the *haecceitas*, the unique essence, of some worldly thing. In the course of the novel Marcel repeatedly expresses his longing for, his desire to sense and feel and know, the pure individuality of what he encounters without "abstract ideas of things" constituting a barrier between himself and objects, places, and persons.[17] One of the wonders of the *impressions bienheureuses* of involuntary memory is that, through exposing that a sensed object is *the singular manifestation of a timeless essence*, the object sensed is shot through with pure particularity, is glimpsed not through the lens of an abstract concept but as absolutely unique. As Marcel puts it in *Time Regained*, the *impressions bienheureuses* of involuntary memory induce "shocks to the senses" resulting in his perceiving, in the memory-triggering things, the "concept of 'existence' which they usually lack," thus making it possible for him "to secure, to isolate, to immobilise—for a moment brief as a flash of lightning—what normally it never apprehends: a fragment of time in the pure state."[18] What this last phrase means is that Marcel recognizes, in light of his reflections on the significance of the *impressions*, that a worldly thing is only apprehended in its true reality, in its "pure state," when it is seen as a reality *both in time and in its relation to its eternal essence*. This vision secures two crucial truths at once: the ineluctable

souri Press, 1990), 77, where Voegelin quotes these lines of Eliot's and affirms their symbolic equivalence to the term *metaxy*.

17 Proust, *Swann's Way*, I: 220.

18 Proust, *Time Regained*, VI: 264.

reality of the unique thing or place or person (since it is no longer known as merely a "conceptual abstraction"), and the *reality* of the timeless essence of which it is a manifestation. Thus Proust's metaxic vision, occasioned by the *impressions bienheureuses* of involuntary memory, secures for him the indubitable reality, and thus the *meaningfulness*, of both timeless being *and* temporal being—and so he can be sure that his own existence has been, and is being, lived in the "in-between" of two dimensions of being that are *both* truly real and truly meaningful.

Now, the sources of *impressions bienheureuses* include, as we recall, not only experiences of involuntary memory, but also experiences of contemplation of nature and worldly objects, and experiences of great art. Accounts of both of these latter types of experience are scattered throughout the novel; and some of them give rise to important *impressions bienheureuses*, such as the young Marcel's response to viewing the steeples of Martinville described in volume one, *Swann's Way*, and the adolescent Marcel's reaction to the "musty smell" in the little water-closet pavilion in the Champs-Elysees described in volume two, *Within a Budding Grove*.[19] Usually, however, Marcel's accounts of peculiarly significant experiences entailed in his contemplative responses to nature and world, or arising from his engagements with art, are described as preludes to, or hints of the possibility of, more profound *impressions*, through his describing them as experiences in which timeless reality is vaguely sensed as a "mystery" beneath or behind the "outward appearance" of things.[20]

For example, with regard to contemplative responses to nature and world, in *Swann's Way* Marcel describes how, as a child, he would continually be drawn by a vague and passing apprehension of some "mystery that lay hidden in a shape or a perfume . . . a mass of disparate images— the play of sunlight on a stone, a roof, the sound of a bell, the smell of fallen leaves," which only much later in life he will discover had been a jejune apprehension of essential, timeless reality.[21] Subsequently, throughout the life described in later volumes of the novel, he is attracted

19 Proust, *Swann's Way*, I: 253–57; *Within a Budding Grove*, II: 87–91.
20 Proust, *Within a Budding Grove*, II: 406.
21 Proust, *Swann's Way*, I: 253.

and invited by such apprehensions of mystery—the "mystery of a place," the mystery of names, the "mystery of personality"—attractions that usually end in disappointment, but which, in *Time Regained*, are revealed to have all along been "presentiments" of the mystery of eternity that is revealed in the climactic *impressions bienheureuses*, and fully understood only by the mature Marcel after a strenuous effort to elucidate for himself the meaning of all these epiphanies.[22]

With regard to art, it is unsurprising that Proust is particularly interested in, and describes repeatedly in the novel, the manners in which art in all its forms can evoke a sense of the mystery of eternity, since in *Time Regained* Marcel will find his vocation in producing a work of literary art—the long novel we have been reading—in whose creation and worth he can now believe because he has clarified for himself, and is certain, that the artistic evocation of the mystery of eternal and essential truth is the revelation of a genuine reality: that human beings, whether they understand it or not, live in the "in-between" of immanence and transcendence.

This brings us to our third topic. It is the revelation of eternal reality, and Marcel's participation in it through his existence in the metaxy, that *alone* for Proust can give his novel its integrative and narrative unity, because its essential subject-matter is existence in time, and it is only participation in eternity that gives existence in time metaphysical unity or identity. The *impressions bienheureuses* not only reveal to Marcel that his existence has a higher meaning than mere existence in space and time; they enable him to perceive the disparate episodes and stages of his life as having an *ontologically interrelated significance*. Thus Marcel eventually realizes and is able to affirm (as related in *Time Regained*) that his entire life—his sensations, feelings, thoughts, encounters, his disappointments and pleasures, his sorrows and joys, his intellectual efforts, his vague apprehensions of a mysterious depth of meaning, his aesthetic experiences, his social life, even his thwarted attempts at attaining satisfaction in romantic love and the ensuing tortures of

---

22 Proust, *Within a Budding Grove*, II: 406; *Swann's Way*, I: 438; *Time Regained*, VI: 508. Proust uses the term "mystery" in an ontological sense, and phrases that evoke the mysteriousness of eternal reality, repeatedly throughout the novel.

jealousy—all add up to something meaningful as a whole, that his life constitutes a genuine *story*. And the central motif of this story—the existential motif that guides its unfolding pattern as we read, and grounds its coherence—is, unsurprisingly, Marcel's *search* for the eternal meaning that from childhood he continually glimpses and in adulthood comes to explicitly identify. In the end he finds what he had always been searching for: "verities pertaining to a world more real than that in which I lived . . . ."[23] And so he describes the afternoon of the five climactic epiphanies in *Time Regained* as "this most wonderful of all days which had suddenly illuminated for me not only the old groping movements of my thought, but even the whole purpose of my life . . . ."[24] And there can then ensue, for Marcel (now merging into the Narrator) the decision to fulfill his call to be a literary artist—a call he had long suspected of being an illusion both in terms of his talent and the value of literary art—by writing a novel about a person's (that is, his own) "search for lost time": his search for the meaningfulness of time passed, time lost, time forgotten, but which in the end is revealed to be not lost at all, because all of its meaning has been preserved and has a *narrative integrity* through its participation in eternal truth and value.

Fourth and finally, however, Proust/the Narrator makes a point of stating, in numerous passages, that there is no proof—no logical, philosophical, or scientific proof—of the fact that eternal and "essential" reality exists, and that we participate in it and can know of it, nor does it matter that none exists. It is a truth whose verification and "indisputable evidence" lie in three aspects, or characteristics, of the *impressions bienheureuses*.[25] These three experiential components are: 1) the *special joy* that typically floods his being in his experiences of "escape from time"; 2) the *feeling of certitude* about eternal reality and about the meaningfulness of this world and his existence that this joy brings with it; and 3) the accompanying complete *evaporation of all anxieties* about the future, "the vicissitudes of life," and death.[26]

---

23 Proust, *Within a Budding Grove*, II: 17.
24 Proust, *Time Regained*, VI: 287.
25 Proust, *Swann's Way*, I: 61.
26 Ibid., 60.

Proust works hard to communicate the elevated kind of happiness, the distinctive joy, that almost always accompanies the *impressions bienheureuses*, by using a variety of expressions to emphasize its special character. It is an "exquisite pleasure," an "all-powerful joy," "felicity," an "unreasoning pleasure," and a "positive rapture"—and again and again, what is simply described as a "special pleasure."[27] At times, he links it explicitly to the presence, and his enjoyment, of the eternal: he describes it is an "extra-temporal joy," a "supraterrestrial joy," and at one point cannot help but surmise that it might be the "boldest" human approximation to the "bliss of the Beyond" of which religious teachings tell.[28]

Marcel experiences many types of pleasure, but this is the only joy that answers and satisfies the search that, as he presents it, gives an ultimate form to his existence. And it is the intensity and purity of this joy that, in and of itself, leaves him without question that he is genuinely experiencing timeless reality. In the joy, the rapture, of the *impressions bienheureuses*, all "intellectual doubts" about eternal reality and thus the value of living disappear; the joy itself is "like a certainty," and Marcel cannot imagine a man who would not "have confidence in [such a] joy."[29] Doubts about what the joy signifies are made impossible, above all, by the fact that every time he experiences it death immediately becomes "a matter of indifference," along with all anxieties about life's slings and arrows.[30] This is most fully and beautifully expressed in a passage from the account of the first, and most famous, *impression* or epiphany, which tells of some of the effects of tasting the crumbs of madeleine soaked in tea:

> An exquisite pleasure had invaded my senses, something iso-
> lated, detached . . . And at once the vicissitudes of life had
> become indifferent to me, its disasters innocuous, its brevity
> illusory . . . I had ceased now to feel mediocre, contingent,

27 Proust, *Swann's Way*, I: 60, 61, 251–52; *Within a Budding Grove*, II: 91.
28 Proust, *Time Regained*, VI: 272; *The Captive*, V: 347.
29 Proust, *Time Regained*, VI: 255, 257, 265.
30 Ibid., 257.

mortal. Whence could it have come to me, this all-powerful joy?[31]

This key question, located near the start of the novel, will be answered only in its last volume: the origin of this "exquisite pleasure" is the experience of timelessness, of the self "freed from the order of time," who can look upon suffering, failures, disasters, death, and the perishability of all temporal things with indifference because these no longer constitute a threat to his search for meaning.[32] The meaningfulness of existence is assured because life is existence in the metaxy: immanence participates in, and is comprehended by, transcendent truth and value; and the experienced revelation of that truth and value causes *necessarily* the instant evaporation of despair and uncertainty about life's meaning.

The four elements analyzed in the foregoing analysis places it beyond doubt that Proust, like Voegelin, offers his readers a fundamentally metaxic vision of human existence: human life is always lived "in a temporal flow of experience in which eternity is nevertheless present," and in which "there persists the tension toward eternal being transcending time."[33] It also suffices to justify describing Proust as a mystic. Most critics have no hesitation in referring to the *impressions bienheureuses* as "mystic experiences" or "mystical experiences"; even Samuel Beckett, so temperamentally averse to the non-ironic use of such spiritual language, applies the phrase straightforwardly three times in his essay on Proust.[34] What is not so clear is what type of mystic Proust is. He repeatedly affirms joyful personal experiences of a transcendent mystery he asserts to be the "true" or "essential" reality; but we do not find, in his reports of these experiences, anything like an "encounter" with God or a divine "person." Although adjectives such as "celestial," "supernatural," and "divine" are dotted throughout his passages explicating the *impressions bienheureuses*, at no time does he ascribe "personhood," in the sense of the Western religions, to the transcendent reality he testifies

31 Proust, *Swann's Way*, I: 60.
32 Proust, *Time Regained*, VI: 264–65.
33 Voegelin, "Eternal Being in Time," 329.
34 Beckett, *Proust*, 35, 69, 93.

to with such emphasis and at such length. For this reason, Harold Bloom describes Proust's as a "secular mysticism"—a reasonable enough description, and one that raises a number of questions and issues that will be addressed briefly in the last part of this essay.[35] For now, however, we need to note a number of existential paradoxes that Proust's mystical account of the human situation, "secular" though it may be, reveals to be inescapable concomitants to an accurate self-understanding of existence in the metaxy.

A first paradox pertains to what it means to come to understand what one truly is as a self who exists metaxically. The paradox is that, when authentic or enlightened self-recognition takes place through acknowledging and embracing the fact that one's very being, as a human, is existence in the "in-between" of immanence and transcendence, this entails at the same time discovering that the most intimate ontological core of the self is permanently unknowable, because it is the element of one's being that belongs to the mystery of what is beyond space and time. Proust makes this point clearly in a number of passages, usually in the context of the *impressions bienheureuses*, by referring to that part of himself that is "freed from the order of time" not as "I," but variously as "a being whom we carry within us," "the being which at that moment . . . was an extra-temporal being," a being that "was myself and something more than me," and, most tellingly, the being that is "the only part of ourselves that is real and incommunicable"—identified, here, as unqualifiedly "real" because it participates in the imperishable reality "beyond" space and time, and as "incommunicable" because it is participatorily identical with the mystery of transcendence.[36] To know oneself truly, Proust indicates, is to know that the essence of oneself is unknowable.

A second existential paradox illuminated by Proust is that we can only come to feel the truth of death—not know of mortality, our own and others, in an abstract way, but bear the full emotional cognizance

35 Harold Bloom, *The Western Canon: The Books and School of the Ages* (New York: Harcourt Brace & Company, 1994), 397.
36 Proust, *Time Regained*, VI: 262, 264–65; *Sodom and Gomorrah*, IV: 210, 228; *The Guermantes Way*, III: 540.

of death, and accept with total clarity the "destructive action of Time" that leads to death—once death has ceased to be a threat to the meaningfulness of life in time as a result of discovering that one participates in eternal reality.[37] This paradox is brought out most clearly in Marcel's account of that *impression* of involuntary memory when, returning in later adolescence to the seaside hotel in Balbec where previously he had stayed and been cared for by his now-dead grandmother, upon touching the top button of his boot to begin undressing, he is flooded with remembrance of the first night of a prior arrival there with her. At that moment, through involuntary memory, she becomes for him utterly real, genuinely "alive" for the first time since she had had the stroke leading to her death, *present* to him in her actual and complete particularity—but only at the same time through his suddenly discovering, at the deepest emotional level, that she is *truly* dead and so learning that he has "lost her forever." While this "sudden revelation of death" breaks his heart, it is nevertheless an experience of participation in timelessness, a "crisis which annihilates time and space," although at this youthful stage in his development he has no explicit understanding of this truth.[38] Thus here we do not hear of an "exquisite joy" or "special pleasure" arising from this *impression bienheureuse*, but rather of a "painful synthesis of survival and annihilation"—a simultaneous recognition that death means irrevocable passing ("annihilation") but also an awareness that both she and he participate in a dimension of meaning beyond world and perishing ("survival").[39] Only later, as a result of the final novel's joyful epiphanies, will Marcel, through his efforts to understand the meaning of the *impressions bienheureuses*, explicitly make the connection between 1) the vision of a reality beyond death which removes death's threat to life's meaningfulness, and 2) the ability to see clearly, and embrace emotionally, the always-particular and grim actuality of aging and death.

A final existential paradox worth noting is that the *impressions bienheureuses* revealing life to be existence in the metaxy are emphatically

37 Proust, *Time Regained*, VI: 351.
38 Proust, *Sodom and Gomorrah*, IV: 212–13, 215, 228.
39 Ibid., 216.

described by Proust as "given"—as not achieved but granted, triggered spontaneously and suddenly, and typically when Marcel is in a downcast and resigned mood—while at the same time this "givenness" is in some sense the consequence of Marcel's ongoing search for the meaning of his existence that constitutes the dynamic core of his conscious existence.[40] Are we to understand, then, that the *impressions bienheureuses* are a "gift" over which Marcel has no control and, at the same time, a result of—one might say a reward for—his continually resurgent efforts to understand the meaning of his existence? The paradoxical answer to this, I believe, is yes. Roger Shattuck has phrased the issue well: everything Marcel has gone through and struggled toward, he writes, "has imperceptibly shifted the odds in his favor [for experiencing the *impressions bienheureuses*] until *chance has the force of fate.*"[41] Marcel's lifelong responsiveness to the allure of, and attempts to reflectively penetrate the meanings of, the "mysteries" he continually encounters in things and persons—the "signs and secrets"[42] beneath and behind and within things and people—eventually make it his "fate," his destiny, to attain to his experiences of transcendence; while at the same time, the epiphanies are gifted to him when he has no inkling of their approach, as "fortuitous," as given even "against [his] will"—an unbiddenness, he notes, that serves as another "mark of their authenticity." Thus we could say he "was not free to choose them," but still his persistent search for the mystery of transcendence has practically guaranteed their emergence.[43] One of the paradoxes of existence in the metaxy, then, is that the explicit discovery of the metaxic truth of existence is, at once, 1) the consequence of effort of will and 2) the gift of revelation—or, to put it another way, and as Voegelin might phrase it: the human search for meaning in existence arrives at the eternal truth that is its answer through discovering that both the effortful search and its revelatory answer share a mysterious identity as gifts of transcendence.

40 Proust, *Time Regained*, VI: 274.
41 Shattuck, *Proust's Way*, 169 (emphasis added).
42 Ibid.
43 Proust, *Time Regained*, VI: 273, 274.

Critique of Proust's Description of Existence in the Metaxy

What are the most important ways in which Proust's vision of metaxic existence, of human participation in the "in-between" of worldly and eternal being, differs from that of Eric Voegelin? By far the most significant difference is Voegelin's attribution of (analogically understood) divine personhood to transcendent reality. For Voegelin, human life is always existence in "the divine-human Metaxy," a flowing process of "divine-human encounter," where the transcendent "pole" of metaxic tension toward which existence is oriented is properly symbolized as "God."[44] As we have seen, Proust never symbolizes transcendence as "God," even as he uses adjectives such as "divine" and "supernatural" to refer to the "essential" reality of eternal being. His account of experiences of the mystery of transcendence are notable—considering that he was a Western writer familiar with the religious traditions of Jewish and Christian faith—for their omission of any hint of a divine personage, of any "Giver" of the gifts of the *impressions bienheureuses*, or of any "Creator" of the world that is revealed, in light of recurrent revelations of transcendence, to itself be a "heightened reality" that "glistens in time."[45]

Voegelin's analyses of the history of human experiences of transcendence, spread among his voluminous writings, make it clear why he considers it philosophically justifiable, indeed analytically necessary, to represent the transcendent component in the metaxic complex of immanence-transcendence as a "divine partner" and as "God."[46] His usage is based on historical records that communicate insights resulting from mystical experiences across the world's cultures which reveal a process

44 See Eric Voegelin, *Order and History, Volume IV: The Ecumenic Age*, ed. Michael Franz, vol. 17 of *The Collected Works of Eric Voegelin* (Columbia: University of Missouri Press, 2000), 317, 320; "The Beginning and the Beyond: A Meditation on Truth," in *The Collected Works of Eric Voegelin*, vol. 28, *What Is History? and Other Late Unpublished Writings*, eds. Thomas A. Hollweck and Paul Caringella (Baton Rouge: Louisiana State University Press, 1990), 190.
45 Shattuck, *Proust's Way*, 124.
46 Voegelin, "The Beginning and the Beyond," 179.

of *increasingly differentiated apprehensions and appreciations of the nature* of the transcendent "goal" of, or "answer" to, the human search for the meaning of existence; and for Voegelin, the Judeo-Christian differentiations, and especially the differentiated insights deriving from the epiphany of Christ and the Pauline articulation of its meaning, have "unfolded" to the fullest degree possible the meaning of the metaxic "movement in reality" that is human existence. This most complete, most refined, mystical differentiation has revealed transcendence to be the God of "loving grace" who has Created the cosmos and his worldly "protagonist," man.[47]

Nowhere in Proust's novel is it explained why eternal, transcendent reality should not be symbolized in personalistic terms—why it is inappropriate to refer to a "Giver" of the gifts of the *impressions bienheureuses*. Here and there in the novel, Proust's language seems to hint at, or take brief, hesitant glances toward, the notion that transcendent reality might be a "divine partner," to use a term of Voegelin's. For example, describing in *Swann's Way* Marcel's youthful fascination with things giving rise to sensory impressions whose power and beauty intrigue him—"a gleam of sunlight on a stone, the smell of a path"—he recalls that they "appeared to be concealing . . . something which they invited me to come and take."[48] This ascription of an "invitation"—which suggests an "invitor"—is intensified later in the novel, when he describes how, as a mature man, in certain artworks he was "able to apprehend the strange *summons*" they presented to him "as the promise and the proof that there existed something other" than the perishable, merely temporal world.[49] There is a summons, which at least hints at a summoner. Finally, there are two isolated passages worth noting. In one, Marcel/the Narrator rather surprisingly (given the portrayal of "love" in his novel) refers to a "universal love" of which his perennially disappointed efforts at loving another person he "knew" to be a "tiny fragment." In another, he mentions a "universal spirit" to which the "portion of [his] mind more durable" than the part of the self that can die should "give [the] love,

47 Voegelin, *The Ecumenic Age*, 314–16, 327.
48 Proust, *Swann's Way*, I: 251–52.
49 Proust, *The Captive*, V: 350 (emphasis added).

[and] the understanding of this love," that he has instead been directing repeatedly and frustratingly toward individuals.[50] There is no follow-up to or expansion on these references to a "universal love" and a "universal spirit," however. Proust's vision of transcendence remains, in the end, adamantly impersonal.

Why is this the case? From the perspective of Voegelin's philosophical explications of mystical experiences in human history, it would seem to be a consequence of Proust's having attained to a certain stage of differentiation—ultimately, an incomplete stage of differentiation—in his analyses of his own mystical experiences. Voegelin refers to both the Hindu and Buddhist *impersonal* symbolizations of transcendent reality, articulated in the symbols of Brahman and Nirvana respectively, as due to an "incompleteness" in the differentiating processes of consciousness in which the transcendent element in the mystical illumination of transcendence is identified and described.[51] A diagnosis concluding that Proust's mystical self-understanding is differentiated to a comparable degree receives support from critics such as Harold Bloom and Roger Shattuck, who agree that Proust's mysticism "aptly compares to Hindu conceptions of the self."[52] What other factors may be involved in Proust's reluctance to analogically or metaphorically personalize transcendent reality—factors pertaining, say, to Proust's cultural milieu and historical situation, or to the peculiarities of his temperament and character, or to the influence on his outlook of literary authors (such as Ruskin) and philosophers (such as Plato, with whose "nexus of ideas" he was obviously familiar)[53]—it would be difficult to determine with any degree of certainty. One possibly significant element suggests itself, however, when one considers the manners in which "love" is presented and discussed in the novel.

Except for the two exceptions noted above, both of them brief and undeveloped by further exposition, Proust does not describe his

50 Proust, *The Guermantes Way*, III: 155; *Time Regained*, VI: 301.
51 Voegelin, *The Ecumenic Age*, 394; see also 130–31 and 402–403.
52 Bloom, *The Western Canon*, 412, where Bloom expresses his agreement with Shattuck on this point.
53 Shattuck, *Proust's Way*, 114.

impressions bienheureuses as entailing love in relation to eternal or transcendent reality—either loving desire as a component in the "joy" and
"rapture" he feels, or love as an aspect of the mystery of eternity that
has "summoned" him since childhood and that is illuminated in his revelations. As is obvious to all readers and critics, the only authentic love,
the only normative love, one might say, in the novel is the love between
the personages of grandmother, mother, and Marcel; romantic love and
friendship are, for the Narrator/Proust, enterprises that are doomed to
disillusion and disappointment. There is, as Edmund Wilson points out,
a genuine "spiritual nobility" in the love displayed by Marcel's grandmother and mother, examples "from which Proust's narrator sets out";
but these examples bear no fruit in Marcel's capacities to properly love
anyone other than these two.[54] One could say of Marcel's intersubjective
relations with regard to all other persons in the novel, including the most
important for his emotional and intellectual life, that there is—to use
Martin Buber's terminology—not a single normative "I-Thou" relationship, or reciprocity of loving encounter, among them.[55] And this extends
to—perhaps to a large degree accounts for—Proust's description of his
relationship with transcendent being. It is a connection with, and a recognition of participatory identity with, eternal reality; but it is not a relationship between Marcel and an "eternal Thou."[56] It could not be, unless
it were constituted by experiences of loving and being loved by what
Voegelin describes as the "divine partner" in being.

If this constitutes a deficiency in Proust's general portrayal of human
existence, with regard to both the normative possibilities of intersubjective relationships and the understanding of what metaxic existence finally means, as I believe it does, the psychological sources of that
deficiency lie too deep for anyone's fully accurate analysis. But it is a
deficiency that can be usefully brought into explicit association with another significant feature of Proust's portrayal of Marcel's existence in

---

54 Edmund Wilson, *Axel's Castle: A Study in the Imaginative Literature of
    1870 to 1930* (New York: Charles Scribner's Sons, 1931), 145.
55 See Martin Buber, *I and Thou*, trans. Walter Kauffman (New York: Charles
    Scribner's Sons, 1970), 53–68.
56 Ibid., 123.

the world: Marcel's almost complete lack of interest in moral consider-ations or judgments, and his total lack of interest in problems of justice. At one point in the fifth volume of the novel, Marcel himself comments on this characteristic: "What was more," he writes, "the notion of justice, *to the extent of a complete absence of moral sense*, was unknown to me. [The extent of my morality was that] I was in my heart of hearts entirely on the side of the weaker party, and of anyone who was in trouble."[57] And this is indeed the only "moral" trait that Marcel regularly, if not consistently, evidences: kindness, and a sympathy for the underdog. But *responsibility* for anyone, responsibility to enact or promote justice, is utterly foreign to him. The only obligation he ever confesses to recog-nizing is the obligation of an artist to his work—including, of course, the obligation to write his novel, which falls upon his conscience with urgent intensity in the latter part of the final volume.

On the basis of this last point, let us make a final diagnostic surmise, to conclude this brief critique of Proust's account of existence in the metaxy. If we were to consider Proust's novel through the lens of what is common to the philosophies and anthropologies of Martin Buber and Emmanuel Levinas, Proust's complete lack of interest in justice; the ab-sence of any sense of responsibility to come to the *aid* of anyone in trou-ble (however he might sympathize with him or her); his inability to experience reciprocally loving "I-Thou" relations with other persons be-sides his grandmother and mother; and his inability to find in his expe-riences of transcendence an affective or existential dimension of addressing or being "addressed" by a God, an "eternal Thou" or tran-scendent "Other," are all of a piece. For Buber and Levinas, the person-hood of transcendent reality is initially grounded in and apprehended through responding, in *love* and *loving responsibility*, to the vulnerability and infinite value of other persons.[58] Every human other makes an eth-ical claim on us because of that vulnerability and value; and it is through

---

57   Proust, *The Captive*, V: 388 (emphasis added).

58   See Buber, *I and Thou*, 66–67, 123–33; and Emmanuel Levinas, "God and Philosophy," in Levinas, *Basic Philosophical Writings*, ed. Adriaan T. Peperzak, Simon Critchley, and Robert Bernasconi (Bloomington and In-dianapolis: Indiana University Press, 1996), 139–41.

responding to that claim by embracing our infinite obligation to every other person (however limited our abilities in fact are to help others) that we come to care about personal, social, and legal justice, and as well come to recognize the reality of the Other who is Infinite, and Who has become manifest precisely through the infinite value of human persons.[59] It is not unreasonable, then, from this philosophical perspective, to attribute Proust's general refusal to accept or be moved by personalist symbolizations of eternal being at least in part to an existential developmental lacuna entailing a turning-away—for reasons unknowable—from the burdens and opportunities of responding in loving responsibility to persons other than his grandmother and mother.

Still, Proust's vision of human life as existence in the metaxy is, in many respects, a profound achievement, and an important testimony in the major writings of the modern world. As mentioned at the start of this essay, modern visions of existence have largely tended to eclipse the fact that human existence is situated in the "in-between" of immanence and transcendence, typically through ignoring or denying the truth of transcendence. Perhaps the most influential and systematic of such anti-metaxic modern visions has been that of Karl Marx. Curiously enough, Proust was Marx's fourth cousin twice removed.[60] Let this little fact permit us to conclude by remarking that Proust's vision of human existence lies, salutarily enough, at an "infinite remove" from the destructively reductionist vision of his relative Marx, for whom there was no illusion more pernicious than confidence in the fact of transcendent reality.

59 Emmanuel Levinas, *Humanism of the Other*, trans. Nidra Poller (Urbana and Chicago: University of Illinois Press, 2006), 29–44; "Peace and Proximity," in *Basic Philosophical Writings*, 167–69; and "The Rights of Man and the Rights of the Other," in *Outside the Subject*, trans. Michael B. Smith (Stanford, CA: Stanford University Press, 1994), 116–25.
60 Evelyne Bloch-Dano, *Madame Proust: A Biography*, trans. Alice Kaplan (Chicago: The University of Chicago Press, 2007), Genealogical Chart 3, [unnumbered pp.] 260–61.

The Normative Flow of Consciousness and the Self: A Philosophical Meditation on Proust's *In Search of Lost Time*

Thomas J. McPartland

We can indeed locate Proust's *In Search of Lost Time* in time! We can trace its antecedents in French literature dealing with the psychology of motivations. We can legitimately place his work in the movement of intellectual history where there was a reorientation of thought towards consciousness, as does H. Stuart Hughes briefly in his well-known study on the topic.[1] More broadly, we can locate Proust in the shift to interiority in modern thought. We can surely see that he has some notion of "historicity," as his characters move to their futures in light of their interpretations ("habits") of the past. His characters can exhibit "thrownness" and anxiety. But for Proust this would be but a bare presentment of the self. Proust conducts a deeper, and more profound, exploration.

The "Age of Interiority" is an ideal type in intellectual history and the history of consciousness.[2] It can refer to a watershed transformation of horizon on the grand scale of the differentiation of philosophy and theoretical consciousness as a distinct cultural superstructure out of a more diffuse culture, whose main expression of meaning was in terms of myth. But just as the differentiation of philosophical and theoretical culture did not necessarily replace the efficacy of myth and symbol in

---

1   H. Stuart Hughes, *Consciousness and Society: The Reorientation of European Social Thought 1890–1930* (New York: Random House, 1958), 384–88.

2   Thomas J. McPartland, *Lonergan and Historiography: The Epistemological Philosophy of History* (Columbia: University of Missouri Press, 2010), Chap. 4.

human life, so the differentiation of "interiority" in modernity did not necessarily replace the relevance of philosophy and theory in human culture. Still, with the differentiation of interiority, there is a new significance and attention given to subjective processes and there are, accordingly, claims of new insights into human being.

We can suggest that over the past centuries of Western intellectual history there is an overarching trend of a shift in the main cultural norm (the final appeal for meaning, significance, and value). As late as the seventeenth century—in the writings, for example, of Descartes and Locke—God is still in the highest place. In the Enlightenment, both in rhetorical power and in formal argument, Nature, often so capitalized, is the arbiter of truth and value. Such problems, however, as the naturalistic fallacy led to the emergence of History as the supreme standard of appeal, starting in the Enlightenment period itself (Progressivism, Burke, and Herder) and dominating much of the nineteenth century with various philosophies and ideologies of history (Comte, Hegel, Marx). But by the turn of the twentieth century such problems as the genetic fallacy helped pave the way for the Self to replace History as the court of appeal. In philosophy we can trace the movement from Descartes' *cogito* as substance, to Kant's transcendental unity with no content, to Hegel's differentiation of substance and subject, to Kierkegaard's "this subject as this self." In fact, we could even suggest that, in a sense, Kierkegaard "discovered" the self. In science we see the emergence of various forms of depth psychology. In various phases of romanticism in painting, music, and literature we have explorations of the uniqueness of the self. Proust has a sophistication that goes beyond even these explorations. We can capture this whole movement into interiority in Bernard Lonergan's crisp formula "from object as object, to subject as object, to subject as subject."[3] And it is here precisely with the subject as subject where we find Proust.

In Search of Lost Time is, in fact, a work *sui generis*. As Proust himself tells us through the narrator of his novel, the creation of genius

---

3   Bernard Lonergan, *Phenomenology and Logic: The Boston College Lectures on Mathematical Logic and Existentialism*, vol. 18, *Collected Works of Bernard Lonergan*, ed. Philip J. McShane (Toronto: University of Toronto Press, 2001), 214–15, 314–17.

builds upon the achievement of the age but goes beyond it. A work of genius spawns its own posterity—but still stands above it.[4] The true masterpiece offers us its own world, a world with its own inner consistency, harmony, and beauty. What an utterly distinct world we find in Proust's great novel! In terms of form, we have the most exquisite, poetically rich expressions mixed in with incredible details from art, botany, and politics, all in long-flowing sentences doing justice to the flow of consciousness itself, combining the deftest employment of modern language with extended Homeric similes. Nothing may happen in the "plot" for hundreds of pages, but we can be entranced by the power of the language itself—while in terms of substance, we have a profound exploration of the depths of the self and its consciousness. Given the nature of this masterpiece no commentary, literary or otherwise, can come close to doing it justice. If this is the case, a philosophical commentary must humbly take the form of a philosophical meditation.[5] And even such a philosophical meditation can but be a simple philosophical invitation to participate in the work itself.

Consciousness

At almost the same time period as Proust was writing his novel, Edmund Husserl was developing an entirely new approach to philosophy, refusing to reduce human consciousness to some kind of material object as in scientism and positivism. Husserl's phenomenology legitimated consciousness as its own data for inquiry alongside the data of sensation, the latter being the sole focus of the natural sciences. Proust gives us, throughout his entire enterprise, covering seven volumes and more than

4   Proust, *Within a Budding Grove*, II: 143.
5   Voegelin, of course, relies heavily on philosophical meditations in his later work. But in a much earlier work, he performs a reflection on his own youthful experiences of powerful images and symbols in the manner of Proust, calling it explicitly a "remembrance of things past." See Eric Voegelin, *Anamnesis: On the Theory of History and Politics*, vol. 6 of *The Collected Works of Eric Voegelin*, trans. M. J. Hanak based upon the abbreviated version originally translated by Gerhart Niemeyer, ed. David Walsh (Columbia: University of Missouri Press, 2002), Chaps. 1 and 3.

a million words, his own "practiced" phenomenology. Without the need for any technical tools or terms we, the readers, experience the phenomenology: we participate in the flow of the narrator's consciousness and its contents. The famous opening scene lets us enter the consciousness of the narrator in bed:

> For a long time I would go to bed early. Sometimes, the candle barely out, my eyes closed so quickly that I did not have time to tell myself: "I'm falling asleep." And half an hour later the thought that it was time to look for sleep would awaken me; I would make as if to put away the book which I imagined was still in my hands, and to blow out the light; I had gone on thinking, while I was asleep, about what I had just been reading, but these thoughts had taken a rather peculiar turn; it seemed to me that I myself was the immediate subject of my book: a church, a quartet, the rivalry between François I and Charles V.[6]

The narrator is falling asleep. We notice his murky consciousness at awakening. His thinking that he has yet to fall asleep merges with dream images of reading his book, now about him and his relation to a collage of objects, a church, a quartet, an historical rivalry. We feel this same murky awakening as we enter the world of the novel and the horizon of the narrator. We notice, too, the frequent references to a salient theme: "for a long time"; "I did not have time"; "it was time."

The consciousness extends to the room. In a reflection reminiscent of Bergson's philosophy of pointing to the motion of things beyond our static and frozen concepts, the narrator relates in vivid detail how he struggles to establish the profile of the room:

> Perhaps the immobility of the things that surround us is forced upon them by our conviction that they are themselves and not anything else, by the immobility of our conception of them. For it always happened that when I awoke like this, and my

6   Proust, *Swann's Way*, I: 1.

mind struggled in an unsuccessful attempt to discover where I was, everything revolved around me through the darkness: things, places, years. My body, still too heavy with sleep to move, would endeavour to construe from the pattern of its tiredness the position of its various limbs, in order to deduce therefrom the direction of the wall, the location of the furniture, to piece together and give a name to the house in which it lay.[7]

The narrator's consciousness is an incarnate consciousness. His very bodily—conscious—presence orients him to get a "feel" for the features of the room and eventually of the house itself. Once he identifies the house, he can, of course, recall all sorts of associations and broaden his imagination.

So the phenomenological profile goes beyond the room in space and beyond the moment in time. As he asks what time it is, he hears the whistles of trains, now near, now far, which connect him with images of travelers on the trains and, remarkably, lets him enter the phenomenological horizon of such a traveler:

I could ask myself what time it could be; I could hear the whistling of trains, which, now nearer and now further off, punctuating the distance like a note of a bird in a forest, showed me in perspective the deserted countryside through which a traveler is hurrying towards a nearby station; and the path he is taking will be engraved in his memory by the excitement induced by strange surroundings, by unaccustomed activities, by the conversation he has had and the farewells exchanged beneath an unfamiliar lamp that still echo in his ears amid the silence of the night, and by the happy prospect of being home again.[8]

The narrator's consciousness now expands to imagining memories (back in time) of the imagined traveler! He also, in the visages of a girl in his

7 Ibid., 5.
8 Ibid., 1–2.

dreams, is reminded of features of women whom he had known at different times in waking hours.[9] He is transported in waking consciousness to different rooms in different houses in which he had slept at different times.[10] What poignant phenomenological descriptions! And these are not just incidental to the real story; these are the focus of the narrative; these are at the heart of the real story.

And yet this is only a prelude. We experience the narrator's consciousness of the garden at the house in Combray, where he would stay as a child, where he enters in consciousness the world of literature and dreams:

> Sweet Sunday afternoons beneath the chestnut-tree in the garden at Combray, carefully purged by me of every commonplace incident of my personal existence, which I had replaced with a life of strange adventures and aspirations in a land watered with living streams, you still recall that life to me when I think of you, and you embody it in effect by virtue of having gradually encircled and enclosed it—while I went on with my reading and the heat of the day declined—in the crystalline succession, slowly changing and dappled with foliage, of your silent, sonorous, fragrant, limpid hours.[11]

The garden expands outward to the land of "strange adventures and aspirations," while it likewise concentrates on the image of the chestnut-tree. We also experience the gate—and the bell. Our narrator's horizon expands to incorporate other persons, his immediate family, the housekeeper, an array of guests—including the crucial figure Charles Swann—and neighbors. Beyond the house we have a detailed description of the profile of the town, and especially the church within and without, a description reflecting precisely the perspective of the narrator and linked by association to other images and perceptions. We expand the horizon of the narrator as we experience his walks in the vicinity of the

9   Ibid., 3.
10 Ibid., 7.
11 Ibid., 121.

town, and the persons, landscapes, and events and associated images we encounter there—on the Guermantes "way" (path) and the Méséglise (or Swann's) "way." Part of the consciousness of the narrator, of course, consists of prominent memories reaching into various layers of the topography of consciousness.

One of the most powerful experiences is that of the hawthorns on the Méséglise way, which occasions extended metaphors and luminous associations:

> The hedge resembled a series of chapels, whose walls were no longer visible under the mountains of flowers that were heaped upon their altars; while beneath them the sun cast a chequered light upon the ground, as though it had just passed through a stained-glass window; and their scent swept over me, as unctuous, as circumscribed in its range, as though I had been standing before the Lady-altar, and the flowers, themselves adorned also, held out each its little bunch of glittering stamens with an absent-minded air, delicate radiating veins in the flamboyant style like those which, in the church, framed the stairway to the rood-loft or the mullions of the windows and blossomed out into the fleshy whiteness of strawberry-flowers. How simple and rustic by comparison would seem the dog-roses which in a few weeks' time would be climbing the same path in the heat of the sun, dressed in a smooth silk of their blushing pink bodices that dissolve in the first breath of wind.[12]

Indeed, the hawthorns offer him charms "in inexhaustible profusion."[13] They hearken to the hawthorns at the altar of the church at Combray—itself a kind of conscious center for the town.

In the Guermantes way he experiences the mysterious flow of consciousness associated with another church. He had been awed by the spires of the church at Martinville in a distinctive manner, in terms of

12 Ibid., 193–94.
13 Ibid., 194.

the presentation of the flow of consciousness—perhaps (as Swann was wont to say) reminiscent of a painting, say a Chagall of a village fiddler:

> In noticing and registering the shape of their spires, their shifting lines, the sunny warmth of their surfaces, I felt that I was not penetrating to the core of my impressions, that something more lay behind that mobility, that luminosity, something which they seemed at once to contain and to conceal.[14]

The reader is led by the narrator through almost two hundred pages of passionate, brilliant, and vivid phenomenological descriptions of the two "ways," such that the narrator's moving summation of them is overwhelming: "So the Méséglise way and the Guermantes way remain for me linked with many of the little incidents of the life which, of all the various lives we lead concurrently, is the most episodic, the most full of vicissitudes; I mean the life of the mind."[15]

Characters and Consciousness

In the middle of the first volume of Proust's novel, *Swann's Way*, we enter the consciousness of the character Charles Swann and feel his growing relation to, and then apprehension of, the woman with whom he enters a love affair, Odette. From the inside we follow his complex, ambiguous, narrow, biased, and frustrated perceptions. We, along with Swann, learn ever so slowly of Odette's betrayal. Anyone who has ever been in the throes of an infatuation can identify with the tortured ambivalence of Swann, who suspects—and fears sometimes in an almost paranoid fashion—Odette's betrayal and, at the same time, cannot believe that she is other than he imagines her to be in his enchanted consciousness. Finally, when the veil is lifted and the enchantment broken, he sees her as her original, less than physically perfect, self, and muses famously that she "wasn't even my type."[16] Only later, when we step out of Swann's

14 Ibid., 254.
15 Ibid., 258.
16 Ibid., 513.

horizon, do we learn through the narrator the extent of Odette's activities.

Our massive entry into Swann's consciousness is but a prelude to meeting in a similar way a host of other characters. In a work originally projected as two volumes, Proust's masterpiece eventually became seven volumes. In the additional five volumes we gain entrance to the horizons of numerous characters, some looming large in the "plot" (that is, in their relation to the life of the narrator), some minor characters, including even the lift-boy at a seaside hotel in Balbec.[17] Whence this focus? Well, this question brings us to the heart of Proust's masterpiece. We do not simply know about the characters, as in a traditional novel; we enter their very horizons. In the way only Proust's distinct and perhaps unprecedented use of language can do, we experience the characters from the inside—and for no ulterior purpose. No single quotable passage can convey this; any single passage could bear a resemblance to a traditional character portrait. It is rather the overwhelming multiplicity of such passages that is *sui generis* to Proust. Whatever blemishes, flaws, and even depravity Proust's characters may exhibit, they simply are; they are, just, there. So we, for example, enter the circle of the Verdurins, a narrow-minded, snobbish clique that, nonetheless, is so "there" that we might fear meeting them some evening. Like her or not, we "know" the presence of Mme Verdurin and the perspective of her clan:

> To admit you to the "little nucleus," the "little group," the "little clan" at the Verdurins', one condition sufficed, but that one was indispensable: you must give tacit adherence to a Creed one of whose articles was that the young pianist whom Mme Verdurin had taken under her patronage that year and of whom she said "Really, it oughtn't to be allowed to play Wagner as well at that!" licked both Planté and Rubenstein hollow, and that Dr. Cottard was more a diagnostician than Potain.[18]

17 Proust, *Time Regained*, VI: 82.
18 Proust, *Swann's Way*, I: 265.

Through hundreds upon hundreds of pages we explore the consciousness of the narrator in his relation to, among the most prominent characters, his mother, his grandmother, Robert Saint-Loup, Gilberte Swann, the Duchesse de Guermantes, and, most of all, his great love Albertine. With respect to the narrator's suspicions and tortured jealousies regarding Albertine, we never really learn the truth of her indulgences, along a series of plausible interpretations and reinterpretations. This is one of the mysteries of Proust. Albertine is the character referred to the most in the story, but we rarely, if ever, enter her consciousness! She is a mystery whose "presence" is elusive, and whose "presence" we encounter only through the consciousness of the narrator as a participant in the story. To this mystery we must return.

We know that the contents of consciousness interpret the world. Most of all do "Habits" form the horizon of a person:

> Habit! That skillful but slow-moving arranger who begins by letting our minds suffer for weeks on end in temporary quarters, but whom our minds are none the less only too happy to discover at last, for without it, reduced to their own devices, they would be powerless to make any room seem habitable.[19]

So the consciousness of each of Proust's characters opens up to a "world," and in this world is the interpreted self of the character. This is most intensely the case, in Proust's novel, in the context of the welter of competing emotionally-charged interpretations in the passion, suffering, and torture of love. So, Proust shows, the subject of consciousness can go through a number of "selves" by way of a number of loves. In general, the subjects seem at the mercy of mimesis as they constitute their social selves in relation to others. Indeed the narrator states bluntly: "Our social personality is the creation of the thoughts of other people."[20] But we also experience something through all these various selves and interpretations—the subtle flow of consciousness itself.

19 Ibid., 8–9.
20 Ibid., 23.

The reader is struck by the unmistakable, distinct, portrait of characters by Proust. Are they really "characters"? Or are they, as the narrator alleges, models for the literary painter, even those persons most dear to him?[21] The literary painting captures something both less substantial and more substantial than a "character." The painting deconstructs the model, ultimately making it more general.[22] As the reader jumps from the narrator's perspective to the inner, often complex, motivations of the character—frequently a person whom the narrator loves—the reader, with the narrator, ultimately confronts mystery. Still, the narrator forms interpretations of the character, and, in the extreme for those whom he loves, himself becomes another self in relation to the person. For all the complexity of the process, what stands out is that we have a consciousness—that of the narrator—encountering another consciousness. Does not our consciousness, too—that of the reader—participate in the process? So what is the distinct feature of Proust's portrait of persons? Like a painting, we want to look at the portrait and admire it. We feel a strange, mysterious, "presence" to it. But this is not presence in the sense of being present-at-hand. We are present to a *subject*. What, then, is this subtle ambience that suffuses Proust's work, even for the most insignificant and mean of characters? Is it not a form of love, a love in which consciousness participates, a love that suffuses consciousness as such with value? Is it this into which the characters ultimately dissolve? Do we touch here the "mystery" of personality?[23]

The Narrator and Normative Consciousness

Proust's "phenomenology" gives us neither a materialistic world of objects (reality is not in objects but in the mind),[24] nor an idealist, solipsistic, voluntaristic creation of pure subjectivity, nor a relativist view of values (which the narrator claims was popular in some lower aristocratic circles). Indeed, it gives us, perhaps surprisingly, a narrator. If not quite

21 Proust, *Time Regained*, VI: 311.
22 Ibid., 298.
23 Proust, *Swann's Way*, I: 438.
24 Proust, *Time Regained*, VI: 23.

the traditional narrator, Proust's narrator still imparts a tone of objectivity as he proclaims truths about human relations, love, and even politics as he performs intricate analyses of psychological motives and sociological influences. Still, he indulges in no moralism, even for characters—such as Mme Verdurin or Baron de Charlus—whom we might be tempted to despise. They are allowed to stand with their own consistency, to "stand" in front of themselves—to exist. The narrator has standards of true values and of human kindness. Friendship and loyalty—however much broken in the story—are goods. Thus there is a kind of non-scientistic sense of objectivity.

Still, what the narrator narrates is principally about the narrator. This may seem paradoxical if so many volumes seem focused on the conscious self-presence of other characters. Indeed, we must take this seriously and revisit this issue. For the moment, however, we need to consider what we learn of the self of the narrator. As the narrator encounters the consciousness of others (now models), so we encounter the consciousness of the narrator. He is surely a being massively in search of pleasures. And his pleasures can reach the level of the high artistic sensibility of a Charles Swann. Even so, the search for meaning in the flow of his consciousness is not constituted solely by pleasures and by acts of mimesis and social mediations of selfhood. There is a normative flow of consciousness, the directionality of the meaning of life, and a correlative sense of reality.

The meaning he seeks Proust will not find in the dogmas of religion or of spiritualism (as much as he is drawn to such a tendency in his admirable and distinguished writer Bergotte).[25] But he will encounter the normative flow of the direction of meaning in life in three related areas: nature, art, and love.

For Proust, nature is not primarily a mechanistic system. Nature is the presence of mysterious forces that encompass our physical being and call it to a still serenity. In a scene in which the narrator meets the young Mlle Swann (Gilberte) he hears an "invisible" bird pressed from "solitude on every side" as sunlight falls from a "motionless" sky; he then, as we have seen, smells the exquisite odor of the hawthorns ("invisible

25 Proust, *The Fugitive*, V: 713.

and unchanging"), which remind him of the flowers of the Lady at the altar of the Church at Combray.[26] When he witnesses with a strange stirring of remembrance the three trees of Hudimesnil, he asked when he had seen them. Or has he never seen them before? Their meaning is obscure, but their mystery is alone what he believes to be true, what would make him truly happy. "It was like my life."[27] Even the memory of the roads near Balbec is a lure to which all similar roads will attach.[28] The specific "objects" in "nature" point beyond themselves to a silent, still mystery. Thus this is not mere aesthetic feeling. It is rather "exalted ambition to stay and live there forever." These experiences are "ineffable moments of happiness which neither the present nor the future can restore to us."[29] There is a glorious tension in the narrator's consciousness from the limits of the particular toward something beyond.

It is not surprising that the role of art is precisely to capture, or rather to express, the moment in the mystery. Painting focuses on the spatial dimension. A scene of particular aesthetic contemplation is the bay at Balbec. The narrator from his apartment's window sees incredible, changing visages of the waves, with "their first undulations in a transparent, vaporous, bluish distance," and a diversity of light "that displaces and situates the undulations of the sea."[30] Near Balbec the narrator meets the painter Elstir, who will also be visited by the "little band" of girls, including Albertine. Elstir faces the motion of the ocean and the play of the light of the sky and the movement of people on boats to fix them for all time on canvas as the throb of one happy moment and to "recapture the vanished day in its instantaneous, slumbering beauty."[31] Elstir goes beyond raw material description (he is not an impressionist) but endows them with form; he seeks in his art—by certain lines, certain arabesques, a certain ideal type in mythological paintings—a character almost divine, "Ideal Beauty."[32]

26 Proust, *Swann's Way*, I: 193–94.
27 Proust, *Within a Budding Grove*, II: 404–408.
28 Ibid., 409.
29 Ibid., 410.
30 Ibid., 341–42.
31 Ibid., 657.
32 Ibid., 586–87.

Music, more directly related to time, also goes beyond time. The narrator compares the musician Vinteuil to the painter Elstir. Vinteuil's sonata utterly transports Swann, and a little phrase of it becomes the "national anthem" of his love with Odette.[33] In both Vinteuil's sonata and his sextet we experience in song something "eternal": the "unknown, incalculable colourings of an unsuspected world."[34] In this plaintive and mysterious call, "profound, vague, internal," we have the foundation stones for construction of a true life. We feel intimations of a pure form of the Unknown Woman and such echoes of nature as the line of trees near Balbec.[35] The narrator could not be more blunt: this is the "boldest approximation to the bliss of the Beyond."[36] Thus music gives us emotion "more exalted, more pure, more true," corresponding to some definite spiritual reality—or life would be meaningless.[37] The Beyond is the reality correlative to the normative direction of consciousness and to a "true life" (the real self in its depths).

Nature and art point to the ultimate experience of the flow of consciousness. The narrator's kiss with his mother, his relation with his grandmother (who seems to have replaced the mother in his psyche), his first love with Gilberte, his infatuation with the Duchesse de Guermantes, and his tortured love with elusive Albertine—all these loves (particularly the erotic ones) with their illusions, disappointments, losses, and suffering, endow life with meaning. With new loves the narrator has new selves. But whence the value of the pain? Paradoxically, even "happiness" (which places us contented in a limited and self-satisfied world) is useful in only one way: making unhappiness possible.[38] The "whole art of living" is to make use of individuals (our loves), through whom we suffer, to enable us to draw nearer to the divine form which they reflect.[39] In other words, in every love there is the tension of the particular and the general. Particular love is dissolved into a

33 Proust, *Swann's Way*, I: 308.
34 Proust, *The Captive*, V: 342, 340.
35 Ibid., 346–47.
36 Ibid., 347.
37 Ibid., 504.
38 Proust, *Time Regained*, VI: 316.
39 Ibid., 304.

"vaster reality."[40] In the "vaster reality" we discover the true self, which is neither mediated by friendship nor fashioned in the likeness of other people. It is the self that dwells "within us."[41]

Proust is not advocating abusing others. Love is not indulged in for utilitarian purposes or some Machiavellian artistic romp. Love dominates the narrator's existence. He participates in it in a frail, human way. But love, suffering, and loss point to a larger dimension of existence, itself perhaps suffused with love. All our loves merge together in the moment to an essence common to the sensations of the past and of the present—outside time.[42] So a timeless moment of powerful joy can only subsist, after the people are dead, in taste and smell alone—as in the taste of the *petites madeleines*, the "squat, plump little cakes," which the narrator associates with his long dead aunt and with linked memories:[43]

> An exquisite pleasure had invaded my senses, something isolated, detached, with no suggestion of its origin. And at once the vicissitudes of life had become indifferent to me, its disasters innocuous, its brevity illusory—this new sensation having had the effect, which love has, of filling me with a precious essence . . .[44]

The anxious "vicissitudes of life" had been neither countered nor overcome by Habit, nor even by the created forms of art. The "exquisite" experience he describes was analogous, he writes, to love; and the effect of this love and joy was not, by its essence, says the narrator, "in me; it *was* me."[45]

Would this kind of wisdom not extend, too, to the other characters and to the reader? Sounds also can evoke such memories. The ring of the bell at the gate of the house at Combray when Swann left and the narrator's Mamma came to kiss him still could ring years later at the

40 Ibid., 312.
41 Ibid., 276.
42 Ibid., 303–304.
43 Proust, *Swann's Way*, I: 63–64.
44 Ibid., 60.
45 Ibid.

Guermantes' party. More importantly, the bell could still ring for the narrator "by descending to a greater depth within myself."[46] Tactile sensations could likewise evoke this in-between condition of existence. Tripping over uneven pavement at the courtyard of the Guermantes' mansion suddenly caused an epiphanic event to occur:

> And at the moment when, recovering my balance, I put my foot on a stone which was slightly lower than its neighbour, all my discouragement vanished and in its place was that same happiness which at various epochs of my life had been given to me by the sight of the trees which I had thought that I had recognized in the course of a drive near Balbec, by the sight of the twin steeples of Martinville, by the flavour of the madeleine dipped in tea, and by all those other sensations of which I had spoken and of which the last works of Vinteuil had seemed to me to combine the quintessential character.[47]

There was something common to a day long past (which harbored a true paradise that had been lost) and the present day "because in some way they were extra temporal . . . ."[48] Here was the rediscovery of the "Time that was Lost."[49]

No more is time lost than is the exploration, over many volumes, of the conscious presence of the novel's characters as subjects. We join the narrator in his ultimate yearning to encounter the mystery of the characters dearest to him. In the narrator's own self-revelation in the last volume we glimpse at the mystery of the narrator's true, inner self as the flux of presence in time and out of time—and we also learn of the characters' (and of our own, the readers') true selves.

We do indeed long to understand the elusive consciousness of Albertine. And so does the narrator, even as he repeatedly recoils from her deceptions recounted over more than one volume, and mistrusts her ap-

---

46 Proust, *Time Regained*, VI: 529–30.
47 Ibid., 255.
48 Ibid., 261-62.
49 Ibid., 263.

parent lesbian relations. He knows how she gives herself away when lying.[50] In a manner that might remind us of Swann and Odette during the infatuation phase of their relationship, the narrator tries to investigate her activities, but, strangely, at times the narrator has "jealousy without love."[51] We, the readers, are first introduced to Albertine as one who is "insolent," according to her aunt.[52] Still, there is something about Albertine. We never really get beyond the narrator's perception of her; but even as she is in her most degraded state, as an apparently "freely" unconscious sexual object in captivity and in complete subjection, we want to know her motives, her perspective, her horizon.[53] We want to go beyond the speculations of the narrator. We are shaken by her sudden death, just as we are tantalized by the misinterpretation of a telegram, bearing an illusory hope that she is still alive.[54] As the ultimate mystery in the story, Albertine is a symbol of our own ultimate longing for the mystery engulfing consciousness.

Proust is unique in literature as he employs his unmatched artistic skills in unrelenting devotion to exploring the *ontology of consciousness* as he portrays the conscious presence of the self and its mystery. His chief value is ontological. It is not, in the ordinary sense, "ethical." Nor is his explication of the normative dimension of conscious selfhood, in any ordinary sense, "religious." Perhaps in this he is similar to Heidegger, who in his *Letter on Humanism* eschewed ordinary ethical claims and onto-theological claims. For him, the meaning of the term "God" had to be determined by the essence of the "divine," and the essence of the "divine" had to be determined by the essence of the "sacred," and the essence of the "sacred" had to be determined by the truth of "being."[55] Proust in his own masterful way explores being.

50 Proust, *The Fugitive*, V: 677–78.
51 Proust, *The Captive*, V: 16–30.
52 Proust, *Within a Budding Grove*, II: 237–38.
53 The narrator mentions subjecting women well before the actual episode with Albertine. Ibid., 188.
54 Proust, *The Fugitive*, V: 642, 869, 889.
55 Martin Heidegger, *Letter on Humanism*; in *The Existentialist Tradition*, ed. Nino Langiulli (Garden City, New York: Doubleday and Co., Anchor Books, 1971), 204–45.

We are called by Proust to experience our own consciousnesses in the tension between the here and now and the mystery of existence in the depths. The trail of memory leads to an event in time, losing all gloss and extrinsic interpretation. It stands alone as participating in something—mysteriously—beyond it. This is the inner—true—self: consciousness in time and out of time.

Just as we must listen to the sonata and enter into the world of the painting to grasp the meanings of these works of art, so with Proust's masterpiece no literary criticism, no philosophical analysis, can substitute for experiencing the rapture at seeing the hawthorn and the trees, the joy at tasting the *petites madeleines* and hearing the bell at the gate, the enchantment at seeing the band of girls at Balbec, and the horrible shock at the announcement that Albertine has departed.

Imprisonment and Freedom: Resisting and Embracing the Tension of Existence in Marcel Proust's *In Search of Lost Time*

Paulette Kidder

The magic of the saving Word is as dependent on man's openness to the order of love as is the magic of the disordering word on his inclination to resist and hate truth.
—Eric Voegelin, "Wisdom and the Magic of the Extreme: A Meditation"

Beneath the outward appearance of the woman, it is to these invisible forces with which she is incidentally accompanied that we address ourselves as to obscure deities. It is they whose good will is necessary to us, with whom we seek to establish contact without finding any positive pleasure in it. The woman herself, during our assignation with her, does little more than put us in touch with these goddesses.
—Marcel Proust, *Sodom and Gomorrah*

A work in which there are theories is like an object which still has its price-tag on it.
—Marcel Proust, *Time Regained*

Introduction

In a story that begins with his childhood, Proust's narrator Marcel searches for what he calls time that has been lost; he finally regains that lost time in the final volume as a middle-aged man when he experiences a life-altering epiphany. Vivid memories of his life flood through him, and after reflection on their meaning, he embraces his long-deferred vocation as an artist. What it means to Marcel to lose and regain time is an enticing mystery at the heart of Proust's work, and the power and beauty of Proust's excited descriptions of the moments in which Marcel "regains" time underscore the importance of the themes of *temps perdu* and *temps retrouvé*.

The regaining of time occurs through a series of *"impressions bienheureuses,"* or what can be translated as "blessed (happy) impressions"[1] or "privileged moments."[2] These are moments of involuntary memory, triggered by an encounter with a physical object or sensation (a sight, a touch, a sound, etc.). In these moments, a vivid reminiscence floods Marcel's being, accompanied by intense feelings of joy, peace, and certainty, and sometimes also of grief, guilt, and pain. Commentators have identified eleven or more such moments that occur over the course of the novels, the most iconic being the tasting of a madeleine dipped in linden tea, and the most extended being the culminating recovery of lost time in the final novel, a recovery that begins when Marcel stumbles upon uneven paving stones and finds himself flooded with memories.[3]

Charles Embry has insightfully demonstrated the ways that Eric Voegelin's approach to literature, and in particular Voegelin's accounts of participation, the in-between (metaxy), remembrance, and the primary experience of the cosmos can fruitfully guide a reading of Proust's account of time lost and regained. As Embry writes, "In the presence of the blessed impressions evoked by an in-itself-insignificant material object, Marcel experiences overwhelming feelings of joy and happiness that bring with them a compact sense of wholeness—cosmos—similar

---

1   Charles R. Embry, "The Truth of the Novel: Marcel Proust's *À la recherche du temps perdu,*" in Charles R. Embry, editor, *Voegelinian Readings of Modern Literature* (Columbia, MO: University of Missouri Press, 2011), 213.

2   Rosa Slegers, *Courageous Vulnerability: Ethics and Knowledge in Proust, Marcel, Bergson, and James* (Leiden: Brill, 2010), 11.

3   For a list of instances of "blessed impressions" throughout *In Search of Lost Time,* see Embry, "The Truth of The Novel," 236, endnote 44. Compare the list in Roger Shattuck, *Proust's Way: A Field Guide to In Search of Lost Time* (New York: W.W. Norton and Company, 2000), 259–62.

to those that engendered the formation of Cosmological myth, which then undergirds the development of philosophy."[4] Embry identifies Proust's "blessed impressions" with the recovery of the primary experience of the cosmos, of which Voegelin wrote, "In this experience of the cosmos, neither the impression nor the reception of reality is dully factual. It rather is alive with the meaning of a spiritual event, for the impression is revelatory of the divine mystery, while the reception responds to the revelatory component by cognition of faith."[5] Regaining his early experiences is for Marcel a way of regaining his faith in his own creativity, and as a result he sets out to write the novel that the reader has just finished reading, a novel that expresses those "rare and dispersed-over-a-lifetime moments that dominate our lives—that communicate to us that life is worth living."[6]

I find compelling Embry's connection of the blessed impressions or privileged moments in Proust to a recovery of a primary experience of the cosmos in Voegelin's sense. For Voegelin, the primary experience of the cosmos is a compact, mythological, and undifferentiated sense of the order that underlies the cosmos and gives it meaning. It precedes the differentiations of consciousness that occur in the major historical developments in philosophy, theology, and politics. Voegelin describes the primary experience of the cosmos as

> the experience of an underlying, intangible embracingness, from a something that can supply existence, consubstantiality, and order to all areas of reality even though it does not itself belong as an existent thing to any one of these areas. The cosmos is not a thing among others; it is the background of reality against which all existent things exist; it has reality in the mode of nonexistence. Hence, the cosmological play with

4   Embry, "The Truth of the Novel," 222.
5   Eric Voegelin, "The Beginning and the Beyond: A Meditation on Truth," in Voegelin, *What Is History? And Other Late Unpublished Writings*, eds. Thomas A. Hollweck and Paul Caringella, vol. 28 of *The Collected Works of Eric Voegelin* (Baton Rouge, LA: Louisiana State University Press, 1990), 177, quoted in Embry, "Truth of the Novel," 217.
6   Embry, "The Truth of the Novel," 228.

mutual analogies cannot come to rest on a firm basis outside
itself; it can do no more than make a particular reality . . .
transparent for the mystery of existence over the abyss of
nonexistence.[7]

Marcel's experiences of being flooded with joy and peace from an unknown source resonate well with Voegelin's account of a pre-philosophical
experience of cosmic order. Further, Marcel's embracing of his vocation
as a writer is the affirmation that, like the composers and painters he ad-
mires, he has a unique ability to contribute, in Voegelin's terms, to "[mak-
ing] a particular reality . . . transparent for the mystery of existence."

My reflections in this essay begin in part from Embry's comment that
"as Marcel/Marcel Proust demonstrates for the next five volumes [that
is, from *Swann's Way* onward], his life consists of a series of social activities and travels that fill up and pass his time in an orgy of Pascalian divertissements."[8] These social diversions fill the time between Marcel's
early experiences of the "privileged moments" and the culminating
epiphany of the final volume. Embry is far from suggesting that either
the character Marcel, or the reader, could have fruitfully skipped these
social divertissements and gone directly to the epiphany of *Time Regained*.[9] But just how do the long middle stretches of the novel, in which
Marcel's epiphanic "blessed impressions" seem all but forgotten, contribute to a Voegelinian reading of the meaning of the symbols of time
lost and regained? In particular, I wonder how the parts of the novel that
I found most disquieting to read—those that chronicle Marcel's intense,
controlling jealousy toward his lover Albertine and his continual mendacity toward her—can be integrated into a Voegelinian reading of the
work. If the central meaning of the novel is to be found in the "privileged

7   Eric Voegelin, *Order and History, Volume IV: The Ecumenic Age*, ed.
     Michael Franz, vol. 17 of *The Collected Works of Eric Voegelin* (Columbia,
     MO: University of Missouri Press, 2000), 122.
8   Embry, "The Truth of the Novel," 225.
9   Roger Shattuck suggests that a reader can take "sensible shortcuts" to get
     through *In Search of Lost Time*; these include cutting out the majority of
     the sections dealing with Marcel's relationship with Albertine. See Shat-
     tuck, *Proust's Way*, 25 and footnote.

moments," why write three volumes portraying most of Marcel's relationship with Albertine (*Sodom and Gomorrah, The Fugitive,* and *The Captive)* that contain only two of the eleven "blessed impressions" in the work as a whole? Marcel's obsessive love affair with Albertine might be seen, then, only as an unimportant distraction from his quest to regain his life's calling as a novelist, which he loses in the early volumes and regains in the concluding epiphany. In that case, however, why is the affair with Albertine such a central focus of the very novel that constitutes that life's work—why does Marcel, having had his epiphany in the final volume, go back and spend hundreds of pages chronicling this obsessive love affair? The relationship of Marcel and Albertine seems to be more than just an insignificant prelude to Marcel's ultimate realization of his true calling.

Rosa Slegers, in her excellent study of Proust, *Courageous Vulnerabilities,* follows Malcom Bowie in calling the novel's middle books the "eclipsed volumes," and in arguing for the importance of these sometimes "scandalous" books.[10] Exploring the relationship of Marcel and his enigmatic lover Albertine is important in order to understand how all the novels contribute to the overall trajectory of the work. It will, in addition, allow us to provide a possible interpretation of Voegelin's own few published comments relating to Proust.

Three Voegelinian Invocations of Proust

The first comment by Voegelin that I would like to address is a tantalizing remark, in a letter to Robert Heilman, which characterizes Proust's lost and regained time as "times which correspond to the loss and rediscovery of self, the action of rediscovery through a monumental literary work of remembrance being the atonement for the loss of time through personal guilt—very similar to cosmological rituals of restoring order that has been lost through lapse of time."[11] If we take this com-

---

10 Malcolm Bowie, *Proust Among the Stars* (New York: Columbia University Press, 1998), quoted in Slegers, *Courageous Vulnerability,* 11.

11 Quoted in Charles R. Embry, *The Philosopher and the Storyteller: Eric Voegelin and Twentieth-Century Literature* (Columbia, MO: University of Missouri Press, 2008), 26.

ment as Voegelin's compact reading of the novel, we may ask, who is it in the book who must atone, and for what? How will he or she atone for guilt and restore order by "regaining time"? Certainly Marcel has much to atone for: notably, the decades he has wasted on trivialities (as Embry points out) and his indifference toward loved ones such as his grandmother. In addition to these actions, I believe that his way of relating to Albertine is a central example of an action that calls for atonement. I will argue that the love and even the jealousy that Marcel experiences toward Albertine represent important stages (albeit negative ones) in his struggle to ultimately become open, in Voegelin's terms, to the fullness of reality in its unresolved tension. It is at least in part his jealousy and obsessive control of Albertine for which he must "atone" when he regains time, "restores order," and embraces his identity as a writer.

A second set of remarks by Voegelin that relate indirectly to Proust occur in an essay that invokes Proust in its title; they concern the tension between opening oneself toward and closing oneself off against the fullness of experience. In "Remembrance of Things Past," Voegelin recalls his early attempts to find an adequate theory of consciousness, and he remembers wondering why thinkers such as Comte or Marx "refuse to apperceive what they apperceive quite well? . . . why do they want to imprison themselves in their restricted horizon and to dogmatize their prison reality as the universal truth? And why do they want to lock up all mankind in the prison of their making?"[12] Voegelin argues that the "quality of the horizon [of consciousness] will depend on the analyst's willingness to reach out into all the dimensions of the reality in which his conscious existence is an event—it will depend on his desire to know. A consciousness of this kind . . . is a ceaseless action of expanding, ordering, articulating, and correcting itself; it is an event in the reality of which as a part it partakes."[13] Voegelin here invokes a struggle and a

---

12 Eric Voegelin, "Remembrance of Things Past," in Voegelin, *Published Essays 1966–1985*, vol. 12 of *The Collected Works of Eric Voegelin*, ed. Ellis Sandoz (Baton Rouge, LA: Louisiana State University Press, 1990), 304–305.

13 Ibid., 305.

series of choices that one makes throughout life, choices whether to exist in the openness to all the dimensions of existence, in a state of permanent uncertainty, or to close down that process and construct a secure but sterile prison in which to live.

If the alternative to constructing and living in a spiritual prison is to reach out to all the dimensions of reality, such a reaching-out can be fostered, Voegelin writes, by the study of classic works of literature, which demonstrate that the normal state of human consciousness is "self-reflective" and "open."[14] The philosopher, like the literary author, through "anamnetic exploration of his own consciousness," can "recapture the childhood experiences . . . [that were] living forces in the present constitution of his consciousness,"[15] and in so doing, discover "the symbols of birth and death, of a cosmic whole structured by realms of being, of a world of external objects and of the presence of divine reality in the cosmos, of mortality and immortality, of creation into the cosmic order and salvation from its disorder, of descent into the depth of the psyche and meditative ascent toward its beyond."[16]

The structure of Voegelin's essay, invoking on the one hand a self-constructed spiritual prison and on the other a liberating ascent through the recovery of childhood memories, lends credence to Embry's reading of *temps retrouvé* as a recovery of a primal openness to cosmic order. In addition, it points the reader toward acknowledging that the novel portrays a state of disorder that is the counterpart of Marcel's recovery of lost time. If Marcel's final epiphany, and his embracing of his vocation as a writer, represent his ultimate openness to the tension of existence, his earlier experiences represent both the continual pull of the fullness of being and his flight from it. Voegelin has elsewhere characterized the difficulty of maintaining our consciousness of being "in-between" human and divine reality, of maintaining the openness to the tension of existence: "We remain in the 'in-between,' in a temporal flow of experience in which eternity is nevertheless present. This flow cannot be dissected into a past, a present, and a future of world-time . . . The concept

14   Ibid., 309.
15   Ibid., 313, 314.
16   Ibid., 312.

most suitable to express the presence of eternal being in the temporal flow is *flowing presence*."[17] The tension of existence "presents itself in a manifold of experiential modes on the scales of compactness and differentiation, of transparency and opaqueness, of world anxiety and faith, of *libido dominandi* and charity, of despair and hope, of acquiescence and rebellion, of humility and defiance, of self-opening and self-closure, of apostasy and return, of Promethean revolt and the fear of God, of joy of life and *contemptus mundi*."[18] Maintaining the openness to the full range of experience is difficult; as Voegelin writes, "a state of order . . . does not become a possession, but endures only in the flow of the tension of being itself, which at any time can collapse through the slackening and self-closing of the soul."[19] As I argue below, Marcel's relationship to Albertine originates in the desire to be open toward the fullness of being, but collapses into a state of resistance and closure against that fullness.

A third passage in Voegelin that relates indirectly to Proust occurs in his essay, "On Henry James's *Turn of the Screw*." Voegelin here writes of artists such as Piranesi and Kafka who symbolize the loss of the open cosmos as "the prison without hope . . . The man who contracts himself to a Self can be so much aware of the open world outside that he symbolizes his own state as incarceration. He is not afflicted with blindness for the open cosmos, but deforms its reality while being conscious of deforming it."[20] Such a refusal to participate in the openness of existence is seen, Voegelin argues, in Nietzsche's "refusal to participate in the reality of the divinely ordered cosmos, his refusal to open himself to Grace . . ."[21] Voegelin stresses here that the openness to the fullness of

---

17 Eric Voegelin, "Eternal Being in Time," in Voegelin, *Anamnesis: On the Theory of History and Politics*, vol. 6 of *The Collected Works of Eric Voegelin*, trans. M. J. Hanak based upon the abbreviated version originally translated by Gerhart Niemeyer, ed. David Walsh (Columbia, MO: University of Missouri Press, 2002), 329.
18 Ibid., 330.
19 Ibid., 323.
20 Eric Voegelin, "On Henry James's *Turn of the Screw*," in Voegelin, *Published Essays 1966–1985*, 163.
21 Ibid.,

experience is not a possession but an activity, and that it can too easily be lost through a refusal of grace, a deformation or contraction of reality, so that consciousness becomes a prison rather than a state of freedom. While Voegelin does not mention Proust here along with Kafka and Piranesi, it is easy to see that Marcel's relationship with Albertine constitutes a literary "prison without hope" that contrasts with the openness of the final epiphany in *Time Regained*. In *The Captive,* as we shall see, Marcel imprisons both Albertine and himself through a misinterpretation of the meaning of the invitation to love another person. He has chosen, in Voegelin's terms, *libido dominandi* over charity, anxiety over faith, despair over hope.

Sodom and Gomorrah:
The counterpart of a "blessed" moment

Let us turn now to a key passage in *Sodom and Gomorrah* (Part 2, Chapter 4). At this point in the novel as a whole, Marcel has taken the reader through a series of stories of characters whose relationships are dominated by jealous longing. These include Marcel himself, in his childhood longing for the goodnight kiss that his mother sometimes failed to give him so she could remain with her dinner guests; Swann, in his obsessive love for Odette; Saint-Loup in his love of Rachel; Baron de Charlus in his love of Morel, and Marcel again in his love of Gilberte Swann. For Marcel, the thought that Albertine loves others, and especially the thought that she has women lovers, brings back memories of these previous longings:

> It was Trieste, it was that unknown world in which I could
> feel that Albertine took a delight, in which were her mem-
> ories, her friendships, her childhood loves, that exhaled that
> hostile, inexplicable atmosphere, like the atmosphere that
> used to float up to my bedroom at Combray, from the din-
> ing-room in which I could hear, talking and laughing with
> strangers amid the clatter of knives and forks, Mamma who
> would not be coming upstairs to say good-night to me; like
> the atmosphere that, for Swann, had filled the houses to

which Odette went at night in search of inconceivable
joys.[22]

Note that this passage shows that for Marcel, when one is in love with
someone, one longs to be a participant in all of the beloved's experiences;
one is jealous of those "inconceivable joys," those enjoyable experiences
and memories that the beloved has enjoyed but from which the lover has
been excluded. This longing, I believe, is a form of the *eros* that draws
one beyond oneself and that reflects, in Voegelin's terms, an ultimate
longing for the transcendent. But the way that Marcel (like the other
characters in the novel) appropriates this *eros* is through a series of mis-
steps in his spiritual journey.

At the end of *Sodom and Gomorrah*, Marcel has been seeing Albertine romantically but has decided to break up with her. By chance, he
learns from a remark of Albertine's that she has had a long and close
friendship with a woman, Mlle. Vinteuil, whom he knows to have women
lovers. Marcel had previously suspected that Albertine had women
lovers, but he had suppressed these suspicions. When he learns of her
friendship with Mlle. Vinteuil, "an image stirred in my heart, an image
which I had kept in reserve for so many years that even if I had been
able to guess, when I stored it up long ago, that it had a noxious power,
I should have supposed that in the course of time it had entirely lost it;
preserved alive in the depths of my being . . ."[23] This is the image of
Mlle. Vinteuil and her lover, whom he had surreptitiously observed together years before. The return of this image is experienced by Marcel
as a punishment, but nevertheless

> from my bitterest grief I derived a feeling almost of pride, al-
> most of joy, that of a man whom the shock he has just re-
> ceived has carried at a bound to a point to which no voluntary
> effort could have brought him . . . It was doubtless something
> akin to what I had just learned, something akin to Albertine's
> friendship with Mlle. Vinteuil, something which my mind

22 Proust, *Sodom and Gomorrah,* IV: 710.
23 Proust, *Sodom and Gomorrah,* IV: 702.

would never have been capable of inventing, that I had obscurely apprehended . . . It is often simply from lack of creative imagination that we do not go far enough in suffering. And the most terrible reality brings us, at the same time as suffering, the joy of a great discovery, because it merely gives a new and clear form to what we have long been ruminating without suspecting it.[24]

This passage in *Sodom and Gomorrah* is not normally counted by commentators among the "blessed" or "privileged" moments of Marcel's narrative. However, this episode shares many key characteristics with the involuntary memories that constitute the "blessed impressions." Like the "blessed impressions," it involves a sudden, unexpected, vivid, involuntary memory; it is triggered by a chance event (Albertine's comments); it is accompanied by intense feelings of joy and of certainty, and it leads Marcel to reflect seriously upon his life's course.

Marcel's discovery of Albertine's friendship with Mlle. Vinteuil, then, is a moment akin to the "blessed impressions." To support this point more fully, let us examine the striking parallels between the scene in which Marcel becomes convinced that Albertine has women lovers and the last of the "blessed impressions"— the final epiphany in which Marcel "regains" lost time through a series of involuntary memories and through his ensuing meditations upon them. In *Time Regained*, Marcel trips on the uneven paving stones, and suddenly experiences

that same happiness which at various epochs of my life had been given to me by the sight of trees which I had thought that I recognised in the course of a drive near Balbec, by the sight of the twin steeples of Martinville, by the flavor of a madeleine dipped in tea, and by all those other sensations of which I have spoken . . . Just as, at the moment when I tasted the madeleine, all anxiety about the future, all intellectual doubts had disappeared, so now those that a few seconds ago had assailed me on the subject of the reality of my literary

24   Ibid., 702–703.

gifts, the reality even of literature, were removed as if by magic.[25]

Marcel notes that what is extraordinary about these moments is both the joy that accompanies them and the fact that through them a truth is communicated to us "against our will in an impression which is material because it enters us through the senses but yet has a spiritual meaning which it is possible for us to extract."[26] The truths that are thereby communicated

> composed a magical scrawl, complex and elaborate, [and] their essential character was that I was not free to choose them, that such as they were they were given to me. And I realised that this must be the mark of their authenticity. I had not gone in search of the two uneven paving-stones of the courtyard upon which I had stumbled. But it was precisely the fortuitous and inevitable fashion in which this and the other sensations had been encountered that proved the trueness of the past which they brought back to life, of the images which they released, since we feel, with these sensations, the effort that they made to climb back towards the light, feel in ourselves the joy of rediscovering what is real.[27]

Both the dramatic moment of realizing that Albertine had a friendship with Mlle. Vinteuil and the moment of stumbling upon the paving stones and "regaining time" are characterized in quite similar language—the language that characterizes the "blessed" or "privileged" recollections throughout the work. In both, Marcel experiences joy, and feels that he has encountered something supremely real that had been concealed from him or that he had known only obscurely. In both instances, he is overcome by the vivid memory of an earlier experience. He feels that the mark of the authenticity of his new insight is that he

25 Proust, *Time Regained,* VI: 255.
26 Ibid., VI: 273.
27 Ibid., 274.

could never have imagined it, that it is given to him against his will.[28] Thus the pivotal moment that leads Marcel to imprison Albertine is strongly parallel to the pivotal moment that leads him to become an artist (as it is to the earlier "blessed" moments).

Marcel's newfound belief that Albertine is lesbian causes him to give up the idea of breaking up with her. The thought of Albertine's spending time with attractive women fills him with dismay and he feels compelled to prevent it. Marcel believes that his jealousy of Albertine is the primary cause of his renewed love for her: "But if something brings about a violent change in the position of that soul in relation to us, shows us that it is in love with others and not with us, then by the beating of our shattered heart we feel that it is not a few feet away from us but within us that the beloved creature was."[29] Instead of breaking off the relationship, he embarks on a campaign to deceive and manipulate Albertine into moving with him to Paris and then into his apartment. In *The Captive*, Marcel chronicles the months that Albertine spends as virtually his prisoner in Paris. Before she finally leaves him, he indulges in elaborate plans to control her thoughts, feelings, and actions, which he wishes were directed only toward himself. He employs spies to follow her and continues to tell her lies.

In an especially disturbing sequence, the narrator describes the way he enjoys Albertine most when she is sleeping.

> I could take her head, lift it up, press her face to my lips, put her arms round my neck, and she would continue to sleep, like a watch that never stops, like an animal that stays in whatever position you put it in, like a climbing plant, a convolvulus which continues to thrust out its tendrils whatever support you give it. Only her breathing was altered by each touch of

28 The passages in which Marcel wanders from room to room in order to pursue his reflections on the nature of time and art are reminiscent of Descartes's solitary meditations. Like Descartes, who concluded that God must exist because Descartes could not have invented the idea of God, Marcel takes it as a mark of the truth of an idea that it could not have been invented by Marcel.
29 Proust, *Sodom and Gomorrah*, IV: 719–20.

my fingers, as though she were an instrument on which I was playing and from which I extracted modulations by drawing different notes from one after another of its strings.[30]

Katja Haustein points out that the scene in which Marcel describes Albertine sleeping evokes Romantic portrayals of one who gazes upon a sleeping lover, an image that in Romanticism conveys the interpenetration of the lovers' souls. In contrast, Marcel's descriptions of the sleeping Albertine convey only their mutual isolation from one another, as Albertine's consciousness is disengaged from Marcel, and "Albertine as petrified surface now forms the perfect screen onto which he can project his images of ideal love."[31] For Haustein, the narrator's relationship to the sleeping Albertine exemplifies an "emotional cavity," a zone "where there is no longer any interaction or closeness, no emotional contact or correspondence between the narrator and the world he perceives, but rather emotional distance and difference, [a zone] where the narrator is left alone, standing before the frame."[32] Haustein finds that emotional distance and isolation permeate Marcel's descriptions of people in the novel, and that involuntary memory—the flood of memory and intense emotion that occurs in the privileged moments—is proposed in the novel as a solution to a pervasive emotional distance. In Voegelinian terms, we may say that Marcel in his relationships to others, and in particular to Albertine, resists the full experience of reality that he encounters in the privileged moments.

Vinteuil's Septet

Marcel's response to the discovery that Albertine loves women, then, is to intensify his love affair with her and to seek to exercise utter control over her thoughts and feelings, to the extent of loving her most when she

30 Proust, *The Captive,* IV: 143.
31 Katja Haustein, "Proust's Emotional Cavities: Vision and Affect in *À la recherche du temps perdu*," *French Studies: A Quarterly Review* 63, no. 2 (April 2009): 170.
32 Haustein, "Proust's Emotional Cavities," 162.

is unconscious and inert, unable to resist his desires. Rather than opening himself up to existence, he isolates and closes off both himself and Albertine. At times, Marcel seems aware that this is the wrong path to take. There are passages in *The Captive* in which Marcel experiences intense doubts about the choice he has made to make Albertine his prisoner. At one point in *The Captive,* Marcel attends a party at the Verdurins', where Vinteuil's music is to be performed. Albertine had expressed a desire to attend, and Marcel experiences jealousy when he realizes that Mlle. Vinteuil (whom he suspects had been Albertine's lover) was expected to attend.[33]

> Each new doubt [of Albertine's virtue] makes us feel that the limit has been reached, that we cannot cope with it . . . It lies there dormant like a half-healed pain, a mere threat of suffering which, the reverse side of desire . . . the focus of our thoughts, irradiates them from infinite distances with wisps of sadness . . . Unfortunately we carry inside us that little organ which we call the heart, which is subject to certain maladies in the course of which it is infinitely impressionable as regards everything that concerns the life of a certain person, so that a lie . . . causes that little heart, which we ought to be able to have surgically removed, intolerable spasms.[34]

Marcel appears to wish at this moment that he could even rid himself of his heart in order to put an end to his feelings for Albertine—implying that he is drawn toward a fuller and less isolated life at the same time that he resists it.

In this state of painful and conflicted desire, Marcel is visited with one of the "privileged" or "blessed" moments that have such transformative power within his narrative. (It is the only such moment from the standard list of eleven that occurs in either *The Captive* or *The Fugitive.*)[35] As the concert music begins, Marcel feels that he is visited by a

33 Proust, *The Captive,* IV: 295.
34 Ibid., 295–96.
35 Embry, "The Truth of the Novel," 236.

kind of genie, a "magical apparition."[36] Unexpectedly, he hears the "little phrase" of the composer Vinteuil, a musical motif that has carried a great deal of meaning throughout the novel, particularly for Swann—associated as it is with his love for, and his loss of, Odette. "My joy at having rediscovered it was enhanced by the tone, so friendly and familiar, which it adopted in addressing me . . . ." But instead of taking Marcel into a familiar reminiscence of a vivid, previously-forgotten memory (as the other "blessed moments" do), the music brings him instead to "an unknown universe [that] was drawn from the silence and night to build up gradually before me." A motif begins, "the most remote from anything I had ever imagined, at once ineffable and strident . . . something like a mystical cock-crow, the ineffable but ear-piercing call of eternal morning."[37] The music comes to fulfillment in a burst of bells like those of the remembered Combray, in a rhythm that Marcel finds "almost ugly."[38] Marcel is distracted by the people around him and by the snores of Mme. Verdurin's dog, but when he turns back to the music, he realizes that the composition is a "consummate masterpiece."[39] He reflects that just as Vinteuil's other compositions had been merely preparatory to this septet, Marcel's earlier loves had been mere preludes to his love for Albertine.[40] He observes that, while other people's ills do not generally touch one deeply, his feelings for Albertine render him highly vulnerable to pain. A phrase of music then calms him and he imagines the living presence of Vinteuil.[41] Vinteuil's music is for Marcel "a prayer, a hope," that emerged from Vinteuil, the unique artist. A joyous motif closes the piece; "I knew that this new tone of joy, this summons to a supraterrestrial joy, was a thing that I would never forget."[42] The motif recalls to Marcel earlier "blessed" moments at Martinville and Balbec.

Marcel reflects that Mlle. Vinteuil is both the cause of his jealousy (and hence, paradoxically, of his desire) for Albertine and also the source

36 Proust, *The Captive*, V: 331.
37 Ibid., 332–33.
38 Ibid., 334.
39 Ibid., 335.
40 Ibid., 336.
41 Ibid., 337.
42 Ibid., 347.

of the sublime performance of her father's septet (because she deciphered his notes for the piece). As such, she is the source of both his suffering as Albertine's lover and his joy in hearing the revelatory musical performance. Thanks to her, "I had been able to apprehend the strange summons which I should henceforth never cease to hear, as the promise and proof that there existed something other, realizable no doubt through art, than the nullity that I had found in all my pleasures and in love itself, and that if my life seemed to me so futile, at least it had not yet accomplished everything."[43]

Marcel's love of Albertine is here explicitly posed as a rival to the possibility that he will embrace his vocation as an artist, inspired by Vinteuil. The "blessed moment" of hearing the septet calls him to express his unique artistic voice as Vinteuil has done. But Marcel is continually distracted, even during the performance, by reflections on whether Albertine is faithful to him. When he likens the music to a "mystical cock-crow," one may associate the rooster's cry with a call to awaken as well as with Peter's betrayal of Christ. Marcel's betrayal of his vocation perhaps symbolically struggles with his belief that Albertine is betraying him, as the two sides of Marcel's struggle to find the purpose of his life are here represented. Hearing the septet thus foreshadows the blessed moment in *Time Regained*, which leads Marcel to embrace his vocation, but at this earlier point in the novels Marcel continues to resist what he refers to in these passages as a supraterrestrial call, "the bliss of the Beyond."[44]

Marcel makes the choice, at the conclusion of *Sodom and Gomorrah,* to construct a prison in which to keep his lover—and himself—captive. He reaffirms this choice even after the intense experience, in *The Captive,* of listening to Vinteuil's septet, with its call to become an artist and to allow his unique voice to emerge in his writing. In making these choices, he overlooks or rejects other choices he may have had, the most obvious being to break off with Albertine as he had intended to do originally. Within the world of this novel, there do not seem to be other choices when it comes to love relationships, for all the central male

43   Ibid., 350.
44   Ibid., 347.

characters—Swann, de Charlus, Saint Loup, and Marcel— seem to experience romantic love as a choice between controlling one's partner and ending the relationship. However, as I will argue below, Marcel's choice in the conclusion of *Time Regained* to liberate his written work to the vagaries of fate represents a third choice, that of releasing the loved one while maintaining a loving relationship.

Time Regained: Relinquishing control

Despite the similarities between the moment when Marcel discovers Albertine's sexual interests and the moment when he stumbles upon the paving stones, Marcel's response to the epiphany of the paving stones is radically different from his earlier response to the revelation of Albertine's sexual interests. In the epiphany of the paving stones, Marcel states that

> if our love is not only the love of a Gilberte . . . the reason is not that it is also the love of an Albertine but that it is a portion of our mind more durable than the various selves which successively die within us . . . a portion of our mind which must . . . detach itself from individuals so that we can comprehend and restore it to its generality and give this love, the understanding of this love, to all, to the universal spirit . . .[45]

By this comment, Marcel does not mean that his work as a writer will concentrate on proving general theorems about love. Rather, he will seek to describe carefully and faithfully the loves he has experienced, without obscuring their reality under layers of cliché, or what he calls "habit."[46] "When we have arrived at reality, we must, to express it and preserve it, prevent the intrusion of all those extraneous elements which at every moment the gathered speed of habit lays at our feet."[47] But Marcel has distanced himself from the intense painful attachment and desire for

45   Proust, *Time Regained,* VI: 301.
46   Ibid., 302.
47   Ibid.

control that led him to make Albertine a prisoner. In Voegelin's terms, he has chosen "charity" over "*libido dominandi*," where earlier he made the opposite choice. As an artist, Marcel has come to regard his personal suffering as nourishment for his art.

> [L]et us accept the physical injury which is done to us for the sake of the spiritual knowledge which grief brings; let us submit to the disintegration of our body, since each new fragment which breaks away from it returns in a luminous and significant form to add itself to our work, to complete it at the price of sufferings of which others more richly endowed have no need, to make our work at least more solid as our life crumbles away beneath the corrosive action of our emotions.[48]

Marcel has come to realize that his loves have fed his artistry and that the time spent with Albertine and others was not wasted, although its ultimate importance is to feed his art: "A woman whom we need and who makes us suffer elicits from us a whole gamut of feelings far more profound and more vital than does a man of genius who interests us."[49] Even his experiences of jealousy, with their accompanying suffering, he now sees as playing a role in his formation as an artist.[50]

In accepting and submitting to suffering, and in embracing his task as an artist, Marcel gives up a form of the desire to control and dominate the thoughts, feelings, and actions of others, which earlier led him to make of his Paris apartment a prison for both Albertine and himself and to treat Albertine as an inert object. He explicitly accepts the idea that his suffering serves a greater purpose and even embraces the fact that his books, with their portrayals of those he has loved, will take on a life of their own and will be transformed in the minds of his future readers. "Saddening . . . was the thought that my love, to which I had clung so tenaciously, would in my book be so detached from any individual that different readers would apply it, even in detail, to what they had felt for

48 Ibid., 315.
49 Ibid., 316.
50 Ibid., 330.

other women."[51] Rather than dwell on this sense of lost control, he writes, "I had to resign myself, since nothing has the power to survive unless it can become general and since the mind's own past is dead to its present consciousness, to the idea that even the people who were once most dear to the writer have in the long run done no more than pose for him like models for a painter."[52] While Marcel does not indicate that his behavior toward beloved persons will change in the future, he does give up the desire as an author to control the fate of his characters.

Recall Voegelin's cryptic comment that Proust's lost and regained time are "times which correspond to the loss and rediscovery of self, the action of rediscovery through a monumental literary work of remembrance being the atonement for the loss of time through personal guilt— very similar to cosmological rituals of restoring order that has been lost through lapse of time." Whatever Voegelin had in mind by referring to "atonement" and "personal guilt," it is possible to see Marcel's final release of control over his writing as a step toward atonement for the fierce control that he exercised over Albertine and that he wished to exercise over his other loved ones. This is a third option for one who loves another person—neither to break off the relationship nor to exercise domination over the beloved, but to continue to love him or her while relinquishing control. This is the option that preserves a tension between possession and indifference, by loving another person passionately while preserving a kind of spiritual detachment.

In *Courageous Vulnerability,* Rosa Slegers argues that, while Proust's narrator finds in his final epiphany the courage to embrace his *artistic* vocation, he ultimately fails as a *moral* agent because he never changes his behavior toward his loved ones. Throughout the novels, Proust's narrator sees his friends and loved ones only as the occasions of his own "feelings, projections, and idealizations," just as his characters project their own feelings and ideas upon one another.[53] The narrator has the opportunity, for example when he experiences the "privileged moment" that leads him to grieve for his grandmother, to understand his own

51 Ibid., 309.
52 Ibid., 311.
53 Slegers, *Courageous Vulnerability*, 138.

tendency to treat others as possessions and as aesthetic objects, and to change his behavior by becoming "courageously vulnerable" toward others—embracing the pain of losing control and forgoing the need to control and possess them. However, as Slegers points out, the narrator does not take the occasion of experiencing grief for his grandmother's death, along with guilt for his often heartless treatment of her, to change his behavior toward other beloved persons. He goes on to pursue his intensely controlling obsession with Albertine, as we have seen. Similarly, in *Time Regained*, the narrator changes as a result of his epiphanies, but the change is in his vocation rather than in his interpersonal relationships. Slegers argues that because the narrator lacks a belief in the possibility of genuine love and friendship, he is unable to take a leap of faith (or to embrace a Jamesian "will to believe") in such relationships.[54]

Sleger's arguments are convincing, and they reinforce the importance of reading the neglected middle books of *In Search of Lost Time*. Marcel's epiphany in the final volume is significant and it leads him down a radically different path than did the moment of his realization concerning Albertine's sexual orientation. Nevertheless, Marcel's path is that of a complicated human being for whom the openness to the fullness of reality, in Voegelin's terms, remains subject to finitude, and thus to the constant pressure to embrace some form of self-closing or "eclipse" of that fullness. Nevertheless, in the concluding passages of *In Search of Lost Time*, the narrator has taken a transformative step toward living in the painful and joyous unresolved tension and openness of existence.

In conclusion, I have tried to show that Marcel's love of Albertine, far from being only a distraction from his spiritual search, is motivated by the same longing for meaning that leads him to try to regain "lost time" and that culminates in his embracing his identity as an artist. The moment at which his jealousy toward Albertine is born is described in terms strikingly similar to the language he uses to describe his artistic epiphany, leading us to recognize that these two moments are parallel and that his responses to them represent opposite existential choices. Marcel's embracing of his intense, controlling impulses toward Albertine

54   Ibid., 217.

constitutes, in Voegelin's terms, a closing of the self and a resistance to, even a deformation of, the fullness of experience represented by the symbol of time regained, a fullness to which Marcel ultimately opens himself when he takes up his artistic vocation and when he gives up control of his writings, and his loves, to the vagaries of the future. In telling the story of Marcel's imprisonment of Albertine, Proust portrays symbolically the modern imprisonment of the self, and it is for this spiritual imprisonment, of self and other, that Marcel atones in the conclusion of *In Search of Lost Time*.

Proust's Luminous Memory and *L'Homme Éternel*: The Quest for Limitless Meaning

Michael Henry

We had the experience but missed the meaning,
And approach to the meaning restores the experience
In a different form, beyond any meaning
We can assign to happiness.
— T. S. Eliot, *The Dry Salvages*

"*Longtemps je me suis couché de bonne heure*"[1] is the first sentence of a very long literary work of profound, even limitless, philosophical significance. However, having written this, I must ask whether or not it is true. Since Proust's first sentence does not seem in the least philosophical it is impossible to arrive at any conclusion about my first sentence without devoting a long time to reading the several thousand pages of *À la recherche du temps perdu* from the first volume in which the narrator and protagonist expresses the ambition to write such a work, without knowing how to begin it, to the last volume in which he finally and unexpectedly discovers the beginning. But does the discovery of the beginning at the end of the story enable a return to the original ambition? What elevates such a semi-autobiographical novel to the rank of profoundly philosophical literature?

In *Swann's Way*, the first volume of the novel, the narrator (whom I will hereafter refer to as "Marcel"[2]), young, talented, and encouraged by his family, dreams of attaining immortality as a great literary writer, but

1 "For a long time I would go to bed early."
2 The narrator does not give himself any name but in *The Captive* he quotes his captive paramour Albertine calling him Marcel.

he is repeatedly baffled and dismayed by his failure to find a subject to which *he could impart* "a philosophical significance of infinite value"[3] (*un sujet où je puisse faire tenir une signification philosophique infinie*)—though such a subject will, much later, *reveal itself* to his receptive mind. As time inexorably passes, through chronic ignorance of both the subject and the philosophical significance he might bestow upon his imagined masterpiece, he constantly defers the moment when he will actually sit down to begin the work. Daily postponements mean apparently wasted time that, for decades, steadily diminishes whatever time remains for writing, should he ever actually begin, while his conviction that he is a useless person devoid of literary talent correspondingly increases—until the most unexpected and "most wonderful day" when three epiphanies, three sudden "*déflagrations*" of memory, spark such intense aesthetic life that he finally grasps how his life has metamorphosed into a tale that can become a lasting work of art.[4] *À la recherche du temps perdu* is in part a novel about its own genesis, or, more precisely, discovery, through decades of reflection and searching that culminate in a flash of incandescent memory. After many years of experiences, memories, and intermittent searching for the beginning of his great work, Marcel paradoxically discovers it, as well as his self, by re-experiencing past time become luminous in the intensity of its presence, the moment of insight that is the revelation of the true reality of himself. At the end of the novel his work of art has finally begun.

Luminous memory points him in the direction of the beginning but does not dictate the words of the beginning. How can he truly begin the

3   Proust, *Swann's Way,* I: 243.
4   Eric Voegelin suggests guilt as a motivating factor in his letter of August 13, 1964, to Robert B. Heilman: "Time, then, would not be an empty container into which you can fill any content, but there would be as many times as there are types of differentiated content. Think for instance of Proust's *temps perdu* and *temps retrouvé* as times which correspond to the loss and rediscovery of self, the action of rediscovery through a monumental literary work of remembrance being the atonement for the loss of time through personal guilt." Letter 103 in Charles R. Embry, ed., *Robert B. Heilman and Eric Voegelin: A Friendship in Letters, 1944–1984* (Columbia, MO: University of Missouri Press, 2004), 223.

writing of the tale of how he finally began the writing? Of what has he finally become conscious so that the writing and the plot can commence? My allusions here and earlier to the opening sentences of *In Search of Order*, Volume V of Eric Voegelin's *Order and History*, are deliberate because *À la recherche du temps perdu* grapples for thousands of pages with the problem of the beginning and its accompanying complexities of time and consciousness. In Voegelin's treatment of this specific question of the beginning, he opens the first chapter of *In Search of Order*, "The Beginning of the Beginning" with: "As I am putting down these words on an empty page I have begun to write a sentence that, when it is finished, will be the beginning of a chapter on certain problems of Beginning. The sentence is finished. But is it true?"[5] At this point in the chapter neither the author as he writes it nor the reader as he reads can know whether or not it is true. Voegelin's answer to the question as to whether the beginning or the end comes first is "neither," because of "the paradox of consciousness and its relation to reality." There is individually embodied consciousness that "intends" external objects or things, which he calls "thing-reality"; on the other hand, this external reality is not some "in-itself" entirely alien to consciousness but is "the something in which consciousness occurs as an event of participation between partners in the community of being."[6] To denote this community of being—that is, God and world, man and society—Voegelin uses the term "It-reality."[7] In this participatory sense consciousness is a "luminosity" that is "located somewhere 'between' human consciousness in bodily existence and reality intended in its mode of thingness."[8] In this in-between position "consciousness, thus, has the structural aspect not only of intentionality but also of luminosity."[9] As luminosity, consciousness is not confined to an individual human body but has a "structural

---

5   Eric Voegelin, *Order and History, Volume V: In Search of Order,* ed. Ellis Sandoz, vol. 18 of *The Collected Works of Eric Voegelin* (Baton Rouge, LA: Louisiana State University Press, 1987), 27.

6   Ibid., 29.

7   Ibid., 30. He adopted this term in part because other philosophers had already been using it, Heidegger being one conspicuous example.

8   Ibid.

9   Ibid.

dimension" by which it belongs to the whole community of being. This paradox in which consciousness is simultaneously both a subject that intends external things and "a something in a comprehending reality"[10] must be accepted, Voegelin says, for the beginning to become apparent. Therefore, "words and their meanings are just as much a part of the reality to which they refer as the being things are partners in the comprehending reality; language participates in the paradox of a quest that lets reality become luminous for its truth by pursuing truth as a thing intended."[11]

The critical term here is "a quest that lets reality become luminous for its truth." Precisely in its quest as subject to attain intentional knowledge of truth, consciousness is an active participant in the mysterious It-reality; and, as witness to the truth of Voegelin's analysis, by some obscure alchemy, in Marcel a lifetime of actively seeking a subject of infinite philosophical significance unexpectedly becomes the relaxation and the opening of consciousness to a reality and truth previously concealed from it. Marcel's quest for a philosophically significant truth of intentional consciousness is the necessary but not sufficient condition for the graced moments of participation in luminous truth. In one sense the paradox is that the consciousness that does not seek its truth will not be found, but also one could say that it must first be found before it can seek. I say "will not be found" rather than "will not find" because this truth is not something that we discover entirely by our own determined efforts, but rather a reality that discloses itself at a time we cannot control. For Marcel, the luminous revelation at the end makes apparent not only the beginning of the story but also, and more profoundly, the realities of memory, mind, and time. The end and the beginning are preceded by the intentional search that opens into awareness of participation.

Voegelin discusses the importance of the "story" as the symbolism "that will express the awareness of the divine-human movement and countermovement in the quest for truth" and as "the word that evokes order from disorder by the force of its truth."[12] Although the

10 Ibid.
11 Ibid., 31.
12 Ibid., 38, 40.

example of the kind of story he has in mind here is the account of creation in Genesis, the symbolic importance of the story also applies to a narrative as extensive and complex as that of Proust, who was certainly in quest of truth, both as author and in his *persona* as "Marcel." Proust's central symbol is Time (often capitalized like Being and other terms that refer to an Absolute Reality), but there are several related symbols and themes that refer to both our existence in and our consciousness of Time, beginning with "the beginning" and "sleep."

To be sure, the beginning of this work is more than just the first, terse, sentence, out of which the entire novel germinates, but is rather the whole description of Marcel's nocturnal oscillating between consciousness and unconsciousness. The first word, *longtemps,* immediately presents us with the theme of time as well as the decades of events and experiences, thoughts and emotions, that shape what is subjectively perceived as a long time. (It is in keeping with the centrality of time that the last words of the entire work are *le Temps.*) The time at which events occur in the novel is usually rather nebulous, the time of a work of fiction rather than that of an autobiography. What is the "long time" of the first word? Months? Years? It is subjective and is left as uncertain as the semi-consciousness that he describes in a very clear, precise, and fully conscious analysis. Time-consciousness varies considerably in the course of the novel. Marcel compresses periods of months or even many years into a sentence or a phrase, but he also devotes as much as a hundred pages to recounting a few hours of conversations and observations at a salon. When events occur in time is vague: Marcel does not say when he was born or how old he was when he spent summers at Combray or when he met and fell in love with Gilberte, for instance. In fact, he never provides his own age and does so only once for another character, in the very last paragraph of the novel,[13] and he gives a precise year only in the last volume when he says that he returned to Paris in 1914 and again

13 At a party at the Guermantes mansion, Marcel ascribes the difficulty the Duc de Guermantes has in standing and walking to his being "upon the almost unmanageable summit of his eighty-three years." Proust, *Time Regained,* VI: 531.

in 1916.[14] Nor, at the beginning, does he tell the reader clearly that he is describing experiences during his adult life, or say what time was "early" for going to bed, for surrendering to a state of unconsciousness in which he was oblivious of time (even though sleep does not produce complete unconsciousness because we can be awakened and we dream). And, as we learn later, the necessity of his early bedtime as a child was a source of constant anxiety concerning the indispensable kiss from his mother, without which he was too anxious and upset to be able to sleep.

After beginning the story with the fact of his early bedtime, Marcel describes himself as falling asleep so suddenly that he does not realize it, yet waking himself up half an hour later with the thought that it is time to go to sleep. The sleeping man wakes himself up in order to sleep. He recollects that while he was asleep he was thinking about the book he had just been reading in bed—"about a church, a quartet, the rivalry between François I and Charles V," somewhat vague and disparate subjects that, in an incoherent dreamlike way, suggest the church in Combray, the music that plays a prominent part in his life, the servant Françoise (and his childhood book *François le Champi*, by George Sand) and the family friend Charles Swann—as well as, perhaps, a hint of the important and complex character, the Baron de Charlus, one of the noble family of the Guermantes. For the first few seconds of his awakening, his *réveil* (although the word also means "disillusionment"), Marcel thinks that he himself is the subject of the book (*l'ouvrage*, work, or work of art), as he and his experiences are the subject of the literary work he has long wanted to begin. Because he is still thinking about and is, in effect, merged with the book, in his in-between state of consciousness, he does not at first realize that the candle had gone out so that he is in darkness. When the subject of the book finally detaches itself from his identity and resumes its objective existence, he recovers his sight (*la vue*, which also means "insight"), only to be astonished to see only the surrounding *obscurité* (darkness or mysteriousness), which is, however,

---

14 Marcel withholds specifics not only about time, but also about events which for most people would be significant—such as the "several duels" that he casually mentions having fought, without providing any details other than that at least some were fought over the Dreyfus case.

sweet (*douce*) and restful for his eyes but perhaps even more so for his *esprit,* "to which it appeared incomprehensible, without a cause, something dark indeed."[15] Only after reading to the end of the novel can the reader discern in this initially obscure beginning the subtext in which Marcel has thought for a long time about a work of art in which he and his experiences were the subject, although he inevitably became disillusioned and found himself in the midst of a mysterious obscurity in which he could not discover the work of art sought by his conscious mind. When his semi-oneiric moments of obscure but almost luminous consciousness dissipate and he returns to the clarity of intentional consciousness, he sees only obscurity.

He then describes the alternation of sleep with brief periods of wakefulness during which, in another momentary glimmer of luminous consciousness, he savors, in the *obscurité,* the sleep of the room, the furniture, "that whole of which I formed no more than a small part and whose insensibility I should very soon return to share."[16] It is as though his level of consciousness is just sufficient for him to be aware that it is a something in the comprehending reality in which it participates, but not enough for him to realize that he participates precisely *through* consciousness. Sometimes, however, deep sleep so completely relaxes his mind (*détendît entièrement mon esprit*) that when he awakes in the middle of the night he is utterly confused, not knowing at first where or who he is, with only the most rudimentary, animal sense of existence, until memories pull him from non-being (*néant*) so that he can recompose little by little the original traits of his self (*moi*). That is, he falls into a kind of sub- or super-intentional consciousness that obliterates his awareness both of the world and of the separate self that experiences or intends it, until memory restores his sense of "I" and of things.

Before memory awakens, while he is struggling to regain the knowledge of where he is, everything—things, places, years—turns around him in the darkness, which leads him to suppose, as in the philosophy of Henri Bergson, that the *immobilité* of things is something we impose on a reality that is in constant motion, a constructed stable world

15 Proust, *Swann's Way,* I: 1.
16 Ibid., 2–3.

concealing the truth that *panta rhei,*[17] a truth that is revealed in *obscurité* and a relaxed mind. Thus, paradoxically, the *obscurité* is a moment of luminescent consciousness in which the flux of true reality begins to reveal itself. Eventually, when he is fully awake, the universal motion, the constant kaleidoscopic transformation that he experiences in the state of minimal consciousness, finally ceases and things resume their usual appearance of having solid, separate identities. It is as though the natural relaxation of his mind from the tension of complete awareness to the obscurity of half-sleep allows him to perceive a reality in flux that is invisible in the brightly lit and ordered world of normal intentional consciousness. One could interpret this as Marcel cycling between constant flux, minimal awareness, and dissolution of boundaries on the one hand, and solid, stable objects known by a clear *moi* on the other, without being able to rise to true luminous consciousness in which the constant flow of time attains a duration that is the lastingness of reality. Or, considering the structure of the novel as a whole, it symbolizes the focused but fruitless efforts of Marcel to think up a suitably profound philosophical theme for his great work yielding, finally, when those efforts appear most barren, to the moment of seemingly serendipitous discovery of hidden reality.

The beginning of Marcel's story continues by describing how eventually, in the rhythm of experience, he lies awake, resisting the obscurity of the night by recalling to conscious memory life in "the old days . . . remembering again the places and people I had known, what I had actually seen of them, and what others had told me."[18] Marcel's suggestion that much of the raw material, though not the vital inspiration, for the novel was regained and preserved anamnetically during sleepless nights (although he does not say whether these early-bedtime nights were before or after his moments of insight described in *Time Regained*) is the segue to specific recollections of his childhood and the memory of what was then "the torture of going to bed"—torture because of his anxiety that the presence of guests could mean being deprived of the full maternal kiss that he found indispensable for sleep. He wanted his mother to

17 "Everything flows" (Heraclitus).
18 Proust, *Swann's Way*, I: 9.

come to his room, not merely to kiss him in the dining room and send him up to bed, but to come as late as possible so that he could anticipate her kiss for the maximum time. The memorable night of "victory" over his parents—when, capitulating to his anxiety and disappointment at receiving only a dining room kiss because of the presence of Charles Swann, his mother not only kissed him but also read *François le Champi* to him and spent the entire night in his room, an "abdication" of her and his father's authority—became the event to which, for a time, he ascribed the decline of his health and will and his daily renunciation of the difficult task of writing.[19] He instinctively recognized, without fully understanding it, that what he gained by the assertion of his self-will was actually a loss—which suggested that no work of art could be the result of his intellect imposing significance on a subject, and that his project was doomed to failure.

Sleep, with the rhythms and complexities of its own peculiar form of conscious unconsciousness, is, in fact, a recurring theme in Proust. For instance, in the novel's third volume, *The Guermantes Way*, Marcel reflects on the paradoxical complexities of taking an afternoon nap:

> Before going to sleep, I devoted so much time to thinking (*je pensais si longtemps*) that I should be unable to do so that even after I was asleep a little of my thought remained. It was no more than a glimmer in the almost total darkness, but it was enough to cast a reflexion in my sleep, first of the idea that I could not sleep, and then, a reflexion of this reflexion, that it was in my sleep that I had had the idea that I was not asleep, then, by a further refraction, my awakening . . . to a fresh doze in which I was trying to tell some friends who had come into my room that, a moment earlier, when I was asleep, I had imagined that I was not asleep.[20]

Sleep is a state of diminished and somewhat altered consciousness, but not of complete unconsciousness, and it is a state of being that we can

19 Proust, *Time Regained,* VI: 287.
20 Proust, *The Guermantes Way,* III: 190–91 (ellipsis in the original).

attain only when we are not actively trying to achieve it but are instead relaxed. The more Marcel is concerned about not being able to sleep the more his self-preoccupation permeates and interferes with what sleep he does have—just as the more he is concerned with imparting infinite philosophical significance to a literary work, the less is he able to begin it. Yet even though during the years in which he was living, observing, and experiencing he imagined that he was not working on a literary masterpiece and was in fact "asleep," nonetheless, in some obscure corner of his mind, there was a glimmering awareness that meant he was not fully asleep. He was consciously unconscious because he was engaged in a search but did not yet know what he was seeking.

In *Sodom and Gomorrah*, the fourth volume of the novel, Marcel observes that

> [a] man who falls straight into bed night after night, and ceases to live until the moment when he wakes and rises, will surely never dream of making, I don't say great discoveries, but even minor observations about sleep. He scarcely knows that he is asleep. A little insomnia is not without its value in making us appreciate sleep, in throwing a ray of light upon that darkness. An unfailing memory is not a very powerful incentive to the study of the phenomena of memory.[21]

Someone with no literary ambitions and no interest in exploring the depths of his experiences in search of reality will go through life so completely unconscious that he will never make any discoveries. And later in the same volume he describes sleep as like a "second dwelling" populated by servants and visitors with fluid and uncertain identities, and its own sounds, including bells that can awaken us. Furthermore, "the time that elapses for the sleeper, during these spells of slumber, is absolutely different from the time in which the life of the waking man is passed."[22] A short time can seem long and vice versa, and after profound slumber we can awaken "in a dawn, not knowing who we are, being

21 Proust, *Sodom and Gomorrah,* IV: 69–70.
22 Ibid., 517.

nobody, newly born, ready for anything, the brain emptied of that past which was life until then . . . without a thought, a *we* that is void of content."[23] In Part One of *The Guermantes Way*, Marcel reflects on the "leaden sleep" from which one's first waking consciousness does not include even being a person, and he wonders why, when the self is finally recovered, it is always the same one that was there before, and decides that our surroundings awaken memories that bring back other memories, so that the self is in the memories.

> No doubt the room, even if we have seen it only once before, awakens memories to which other, older memories cling, or perhaps some were dormant in us, of which we now become conscious. The resurrection at our awakening—after that beneficent attack of mental alienation which is sleep—must after all be similar to what occurs when we recall a name, a line, a refrain that we had forgotten. And perhaps the resurrection of the soul after death is to be conceived as a phenomenon of memory.[24]

Profound, "leaden" sleep is the temporary but complete loss of time, consciousness, and self, a kind of death from which awakening is a "resurrection," although in this case the resurrection through memory is a return to the familiar world of consciousness, experience, and personality, analogous to the recollection of something dormant or forgotten in us. The fullest resurrection would be the fullest awakening to luminous consciousness of the reality of time and self. A hint of the desire to awaken to some new reality appears in his observation that taking a new sleep medication stirs up "a delicious expectancy of the unknown"—unknown forms of sleep, new groups of sensations, possibly illness, blissful happiness, or even death. But what is this unknown reality that awakens in Marcel the intense desire to know it?

From childhood he is, of course, immersed—with increasing intentional consciousness—in time, not only in the sense that his experiences

23 Ibid.
24 Proust, *The Guermantes Way,* III: 111.

take place in time but also in the sense that he is surrounded by the ubiq-
uitous evidence of a "long time." He lives in the midst of old buildings,
both in Paris and in the village of Combray with its old church and the
ruins of a medieval castle; he knows families of ancient lineage, particularly the Guermantes; he speaks a language of words and place names
that evolved from ancient Latin through centuries of accreted mispro-
nunciation; he is also aware of the vast expanses of geological time. Furthermore, he knows the relativity in our experience of duration, not only
when sleeping but also when awake: when he is absorbed in reading, an
hour seems like only a few minutes, and when he is seized by an intense
desire, waiting even a short time for its hoped-for fulfillment can seem
interminable. He experiences his inner life as a series of emotional states
or selves, and he comes to understand how time gradually both expunges
grief and renders commonplace a political position that, to most people,
once seemed shocking, such as Dreyfusism.

However, he also becomes aware not only of his constant struggle
in intentional consciousness to transcend the soul and time, "to break
out into the world," to advance "towards the ultimate conquest of truth,"
that is, to master reality, but also of the limitations of attempting to conquer truth, because it means that we are seeking in the outside world of
objects only "the reflection of what our soul has projected on to them;
we are disillusioned when we find that they are in reality devoid of the
charm which they owed in our minds to the association of certain
ideas."[25]

Marcel's efforts to break out into the real world beyond the conventional world merely projected by our souls, or minds, is reminiscent of
philosophers such as Kant and Bergson, and particularly the latter.[26] But
Proust, being an artist, did not simply follow Bergson, whom he had
read, but transformed and transcended him by creating an immensely
complex and vivid work of art that brings time and experience to life in
a way that a philosophical essay cannot. Although Proust reportedly said
that he had not been influenced by Bergson there can be little doubt that

25 Proust, *Swann's Way,* I: 119.
26 For Kant it is impossible to attain knowledge of reality but for Bergson, al-
    though difficult, it is both possible and necessary for the life of the spirit.

Bergson's thinking about time, duration, flux, and memory had a significant influence on him.[27] Bergson had reworked Kant's philosophy so that the reality beneath the phenomena is the ceaseless flow of creative Time that is constantly bringing forth something so radically new that, he concluded, it cannot even be said to be possible until it is actual. The phenomenal world of static things or states is an artificial world created by our intellects so that we might survive by analytically and conceptually stopping the constant flux and freezing it into concepts that make the things in the world predictable and thereby useful. Science gives us reliable appearances, but to know reality itself our consciousness must enter through intuition or insight into the inner metaphysical *duration,* the continuity in the constant flux. Analytic, scientific, intellectual knowledge using static concepts is actually a loss of reality. Furthermore, while intuitions of mobility can be immobilized as concepts, thereby losing much of their metaphysical truth, no aggregation of intellectual concepts can conceive an intuitive knowledge of reality. The only reality that we can definitely know from within is our own self, which endures in its constant flux.

In *Matter and Memory,* first published in 1896, Bergson presented his own version of dualism in which "memory . . . is just the intersection of mind (*l'esprit*) and matter."[28] Our mental functions are concerned with action in a world in which our intellects produce a thing-reality that can be of service for our survival by imposing "instantaneous sections"[29] on the continuous flux of duration in which the past is never lost but is constantly carried forward. In his *Introduction to Metaphysics* he wrote, regarding the continuous flux of the enduring inner self, that "there is a

---

27 Much has been written about Bergson's influence on Proust. Shattuck says that "Proust's denials of Bergson's influence can only be termed disingenuous." Roger Shattuck, *Proust's Way: A Field Guide to* In Search of Lost Time (New York: W. W. Norton & Company, 2000), 115. Aside from the fact that Bergson's work was well known in French intellectual circles, Bergson married Proust's cousin and by some accounts Proust was the best man.

28 Henri Bergson, *Matter and Memory,* tr. Nancy Margaret Paul and W. Scott Palmer (New York: Zone Books, 1988), 13.

29 Ibid., 149.

succession of states, each of which announces that which follows and contains that which precedes it. . . . In reality, no one of them begins or ends, but all extend into each other."[30] Every moment of the past is preserved in the present through memory. Therefore, "consciousness means memory" because the fullness of consciousness means existence in the "It-reality" (to use Voegelin's term) of mobility and duration.[31] This means that in reality there are no *things*, not even changing things, but only the becoming, the continuity of duration in flux, in a present that is "*what is being made.*"[32] In his view the flow of time means that "*[p]ractically, we perceive only the past,* the pure present being the invisible progress of the past gnawing into the future,"[33] and since the past is different for each individual because of specific concrete differences of experience at every moment, no two persons ever have identical experiences, just as no one person ever has exactly the same experience twice. For Bergson nothing in the past is ever lost but everything accumulates so that every moment of the past of a conscious being affects the way in which that being experiences the present. It is not going too far to say that individual identity consists in the duration and ongoing interpenetration of countless specific experiences.

Practical or perceptual consciousness, which includes "the memory of habit" of the organized, analytic world of the intellect, is concerned with action in the present. It may recall past "states" that are useful, but "the rest remains in the dark" (*le reste demeure obscure*) where it is difficult to recall. This hidden past, eclipsed by "the necessities of present action," can find its way into consciousness when "we renounce the interests of effective action to replace ourselves, so to speak, in the life of dreams," as Marcel does at the beginning of Proust's novel. Sleep and dreams mean a relaxation of the mind in which memories that we had

30 Henri Bergson, *An Introduction to Metaphysics,* tr. T. E. Hulme (Indianapolis: The Library of Liberal Arts, 1955), 25.
31 Ibid., 26.
32 Bergson, *Matter and Memory,* 149. Italics in the original. In *An Introduction to Metaphysics,* Bergson says that reality is "mobility. Not *things* made but things in the making, not self-maintaining *states*, but only changing states exist" (49).
33 Bergson, *Matter and Memory,* 150. Italics in the original.

believed irretrievable "then reappear with striking completeness; we live over again, in all their detail, forgotten scenes of childhood . . . ."[34] While pure perception keeps us involved in the material realm, memory, particularly "pure or spontaneous memory" when "a chance event disturbs the equilibrium established by habit and brings back the complete image of a past moment still stamped with 'a date and a place,'"[35] enables us to penetrate into the world of spirit because memory takes us outside the realm of physical and material action. Spirit is "distinct from matter in that it is . . . *memory,* that is to say, a synthesis of past and present with a view to the future, in that it contracts the moments of this matter in order to use them and to manifest itself by actions which are the final aim of its union with the body."[36] In short, Bergson considered memory "the domain of the spirit."[37]

Bergson believed that philosophizing meant *"to invert the habitual direction of the work of thought,"*[38] to think in terms of motion and fluidity rather than our customary and useful static concepts. One finds echoes of Bergson in Marcel's phrases about "snapshots" and immobilizing time, and his statement that the artist's work, the "struggle to discern beneath matter, beneath experience, beneath words, something that is different from them"[39] is a process exactly the reverse of our normal everyday lives. Marcel also sought to use memory to enter the realm of spirit but wanted to do this above all in order to find an un-Bergsonian extra-temporal, or timeless, or eternal meaning. The original mistranslation of the novel's title as *Remembrance of Things Past* conveys the surface narrative of the novel as an account of recollected events, conversations, relationships, thoughts, and feelings from a distant past, but largely obscures Proust's point that remembrance is only the beginning because what is essential is not the spiritually lifeless memory of habit— the "snapshot" memories—but, first, the search for the living reality believed to be lost and, second, receptivity to the pure or spontaneous

34   Ibid., 154.
35   Shattuck, *Proust's Way,* 114–15.
36   Bergson, *Matter and Memory,* 220.
37   Ibid., 240.
38   Bergson, *Introduction to Metaphysics,* 52 (emphasis in original).
39   Proust, *Time Regained,* VI: 299.

memory, the nostalgic yet luminous recollection and recovery of happiness that seemed lost in time, the old renewed in its meaning. And while time flows ineluctably in the physical realm, its meaning exists timelessly when consciousness transcends intentionality in moments of luminosity.

In *Time Regained*, the final volume of Proust's novel, this finally occurs with three sudden eruptions of memory triggered by sensuous experiences as Marcel attends a party at the Guermantes mansion the day after his return to Paris after "long years" in a sanatorium for treatment of his lifelong health problems. Like a castaway who has resigned himself to death the moment before a rescue ship appears on the horizon, just after Marcel has completely abandoned literature and resigned himself to a life of frivolous social gatherings, by chance he abruptly and joyfully realizes that he has found both the infinitely valuable significance (whether philosophical or not is another question) and his gift for literature through direct sensuous memory that bypasses the intellect's futile labors. "The past is hidden somewhat outside the realm, beyond the reach of intellect, in some material object (in the sensation which that material object would give us) of which we have no inkling. And it depends on chance whether or not we come upon this object before we ourselves must die."[40] Past time can be recovered only through the unpredictable irruptions into consciousness of sensuous experiences and all their associations.

The first such onrush of memory that he experienced was, of course, long before, on a dreary day when he came home cold and dispirited (*accablé*, crushed, overwhelmed) and his mother brought him tea and "*petites madeleines*" to warm and cheer him. As he recounts in *Swann's Way,* the very first taste of tea-soaked cake precipitated an exquisite (*délicieux*) pleasure that briefly but dramatically changed his whole perspective on life by filling him with a "precious essence" that, he says, *was* him rather than merely being in him. His attempts to repeat the sensation with more tea and madeleine produce only diminishing results because he cannot evoke the same exquisite pleasure at will, and it is not in the tea: "The drink has called it into being, but does not know

40 Proust, *Swann's Way,* I: 59.

it . . . ."[41] He turns toward his mind [*esprit*] as the only possible discoverer of the truth—even though it seems inadequate for the task—and asks himself what was this unknown state [*état inconnu*] that was so overwhelming in its felicity and reality that it had overpowered all other states of consciousness. After an intense but fruitless effort of concentration he relaxes his mind and only then, when he is thus distracted from the mental effort to conquer the truth, does he feel something start within him and rise to the level of conscious memory, "this memory, this old dead moment which the magnetism of an identical moment" has raised from the depths of his being. Suddenly there appears the childhood memory of his deceased aunt Léonie giving him a "little piece" (*un petit morceau*) of madeleine dipped in her own cup of tea. Taste and smell, more fragile but more enduring or tenacious of life (*vivaces*) than the other senses, are able to bear "the vast structure of recollection" (*l'édifice immense du souvenir*). In this case the memory of a simple taste is tightly interwoven with the memories of everything in his happy childhood, his lost paradise, hence the powerful feeling of *félicité*. This experience foreshadows his much later epiphanies without itself being sufficient to serve as a catalyst for literature, because he did not then fully grasp the significance of a sensation that seemed so fortuitous.

In the middle volumes of Proust's novel Marcel mentions a number of incidents that are lesser madeleine moments: "the cold and almost sooty smell of [a] trellised pavilion" that fills him with happiness because it reminds him of his uncle Adolphe's sitting room at Combray;[42] the sudden appearance of three trees near Hudimesnil that for some elusive reason remind him of something familiar and overwhelm him with happiness;[43] memories of "ineffable moments of happiness which neither the present nor the future can restore to us and which we taste only once in a lifetime!";[44] the sudden "exquisite memory" of his childhood brought on by the sight of a hawthorn bush as he is out for a walk with friends;[45]

41 Proust, *Swann's Way,* I: 61.
42 Proust, *Within a Budding Grove,* II: 91.
43 Ibid., 404.
44 Ibid., 410.
45 Ibid., 684–85.

all of the childhood memories evoked simply by hearing the name "Guermantes";[46] a letter from his stockbroker that reopened for an instant a memory of the long-departed Albertine;[47] a sudden piercing memory of his deceased grandmother awakened by a similarity of his state of mind to his mental state on an earlier occasion when his grandmother had comforted him.[48] These are all glimmerings that do not bring illumination or full insight.

The most important, evocative, and frequently recurring adumbration of insight, or luminosity, is the "little phrase" in the andante of the Vinteuil sonata for violin and piano, which is introduced in "Swann in Love," the middle section of *Swann's Way*, when Charles Swann hears the sonata for the first time at an evening party. He is enjoying the music when pleasure abruptly sublimates to an "exquisite sensation" (*la sensation délicieuse*) of rapture through a phrase or harmony (he did not know which) that "opened and expanded his soul, as the fragrance of certain roses, wafted upon the moist air of evening, has the power of dilating one's nostrils."[49] In Marcel's own reflections on music he sees that it is an art form of constant flux, both of evanescent notes and of the sensations they awaken in us. Barely discernible motifs emerge only "to plunge again and disappear and drown," but memory "like a labourer who toils at the laying down of firm foundations beneath the tumult of the waves, by fashioning for us facsimiles of those fugitive phrases, enable[s] us to compare and contrast them with those that follow."[50] Memory seeks the order, the "design, architecture, thought"[51] in the midst of flux. Swann's memory enables him to clearly distinguish "a phrase which emerged for a few moments above the waves of sound" suggesting "new vistas" and "a world of inexpressible delights" that he had previously never imagined and "into which he felt that nothing else could initiate him." For this single fleeting musical phrase he is filled with love, "as with a new and strange desire." When the phrase reappears it brings a

46 Proust, *The Guermantes Way*, III: 5.
47 Proust, *The Fugitive*, V: 866.
48 Proust, *Sodom and Gomorrah*, IV: 210.
49 Proust, *Swann's Way*, I: 294.
50 Ibid., 295.
51 Ibid., 296.

diminished pleasure, but by the time he returns home the phrase has wrought in him a need, even a passion, for this beauty, a passion that seems to offer "rejuvenation" by awakening him from "moral barren-ness"[52] and from an immersion in the trivial to "matters of fundamental importance," to the "invisible realities in which he had ceased to be-lieve."[53] Unlike the madeleine moment, which is an eruption of specific personal memory with emotionally rich and profound associations, Swann does not suddenly recall a forgotten moment in his childhood, but instead experiences an awakening of sensuous associations with complex overtones of an invisible truth and an immensely desirable re-ality. This experience of Swann in the first volume is a foreshadowing of the incandescent memories of Marcel in the final volume.

Because of complex circumstances, Swann at that time was unable to learn the name of the composer, but a year later he hears the work again and is finally able to learn that it was written by Vinteuil, who was known to Swann only as an old piano teacher at Combray and whom Marcel himself would later think of only as "timid and sad."[54] He acquires the sheet music so that he "could have it again to himself, at home, as often as he wished, could study its language and acquire its secrets,"[55] particu-larly what the little phrase meant to the composer. Further, Swann had "fallen in love with that little phrase" as he was contemporaneously falling in love with Odette, so that in his mind these loves became asso-ciated, and later he often asked her to play the little phrase over and over again, no matter that she played it badly.[56] The phrase remained for Swann a bearer of mystery, a promise of "unknown delight," and in it he sought "a meaning to which his intelligence could not descend."[57] As he stripped his soul of "the whole armour of reason," "he began to realize how much that was painful, perhaps even how much secret and unappeased sorrow

52 Ibid., 298.
53 Ibid., 297–98.
54 Proust, *The Captive,* V: 338.
55 Proust, *Swann's Way,* I: 299.
56 Marcel later tells Albertine that the little phrase "had been as it were the national anthem of the love of Swann and Odette." Proust, *The Captive,* V: 506.
57 Proust, *Swann's Way,* I: 335–36.

underlay the sweetness of the phrase,"[58] even though it brought no suffering to him. Further references to "the little phrase" in "Swann in Love" use various poetic images of women, even a protective goddess, as Swann gradually arrives at the feeling that he and Odette were known to *it*, to the phrase, that the phrase had witnessed their joys and "warned him of their frailty"[59] and eventually spoke to him of the sufferings that he had endured because of his jealous passion for the unfaithful Odette.

In the second volume, *Within a Budding Grove*, when Swann has long been married—not entirely happily—to Odette, and Marcel is grown up, Swann attempts to express to Marcel the beauty of the sonata as evoking "the moment when night is falling among the trees, when the arpeggios of the violin call down a cooling dew upon the earth," and the little phrase is "the Bois de Boulogne plunged in a cataleptic trance."[60] Marcel, who is himself just becoming aware of the sensuous and emotional overtones of the sonata, notes that for Swann they suggested evening and trees because of the many evenings when he had listened to the sonata at restaurants while dining *al fresco* under foliage, memories that for Swann were rich with countless sensations and experiences. In the fifth volume of the novel, *The Captive*, Marcel plays the sonata himself and realizes that it reminds him of "*Tristan.*" He is then struck by how much reality was in the work of Wagner, as he

> contemplated once more those insistent, fleeting themes which visit an act, recede only to return again and again, and, sometimes distant, dormant, almost detached, are at other moments, while remaining vague, so pressing and so close, so internal, so visceral, that they seem like the reprise not so much of a musical motif as of an attack of neuralgia.[61]

Proust's novel is, of course, constructed in much the same way as a musical work, containing not only the evocative beauty of Vinteuil's sonata

58 Ibid., 337.
59 Ibid., 495.
60 Proust, *Within A Budding Grove*, II: 144–45.
61 Proust, *The Captive,* V: 205–06.

(and also his septet)—a theme that returns again and again, particularly in *The Captive* and *The Fugitive*—but also the recurrent moments of partial memory-induced awakening which are sometimes distant and obscure but at other times much stronger and more visceral. In this complex interplay, Vinteuil's sonata itself is one of numerous themes in the novel; other themes include the arts of literature, music, and painting; familial, erotic, and homosexual love; the aristocracy with all its foibles; the beauties of nature; sleep and waking; the nighttime kiss; the idiosyncrasies of Marcel's family's servant Françoise and numerous other characters; the complexities of the Baron de Charlus; and of course Time, to name but a few. All of these Proust weaves into a rich composition intended to awaken in every reader some "little phrase" moments.

In *The Captive*, when Marcel hears Vinteuil's unpublished septet, he recognizes the little phrase quoted and embedded in an unknown "glowing" work that opens to him a completely new realm of beauty. To this experience he devotes a lengthy meditation that is interwoven with reflections on his current painful love for Albertine, and in which he contrasts the septet to the emotionally "lily-white" sonata as a triumph and consummate masterpiece that renders the beauties of the sonata, by comparison, familiar and almost commonplace. The septet, which "extended . . . the unknown, incalculable colourings of an unsuspected world,"[62] begins with "flat, unbroken surfaces like those of the sea on a morning that threatens storm, in the midst of an eerie silence, in an infinite void . . . and it was into a rose-red daybreak that this unknown universe was drawn from the silence and the night to build up gradually before me." The music progresses to "noon" when "in a burst of scorching but transitory sunlight, it seemed to reach fulfillment in a heavy, rustic, almost cloddish gaiety,"[63] which Marcel finds less appealing. This is only the beginning, for as the music continues he experiences the work not only as a whole that is profoundly complex, rich, and moving, a proof of the individuality of the artist, even of "the irreducibly individual existence of the soul,"[64] but also as the interplay between the superficial Apollonian intellect and the Dionysian autonomy of life.

62 Ibid., 339–40.
63 Ibid., 333.
64 Ibid., 341.

> When Vinteuil took up the same phrase again and again, di-
> versified it, amused himself by altering its rhythm, by making
> it reappear in its original form, those deliberate resemblances,
> the work of his intellect, necessarily superficial, never suc-
> ceeded in being as striking as the disguised, involuntary re-
> semblances, which broke out in different colours, between
> the two separate masterpieces.[65]

What is most interesting about the septet, presumably written after the sonata, is the surprising ways in which it transforms and elevates the phrases and themes of the earlier work.

This recollection and transformation, even from the very beginning of an artist's works, seems to be the effort to articulate something inef-fable, "eternal and at once recognizable," something beyond the power of the intellect, even though it has overtones of Platonic *anamnesis*. "Each artist seems thus to be the native of an unknown country, which he himself has forgotten, and which is different from that whence another great artist, setting sail for the earth, will eventually emerge . . . . Com-posers do not remember this lost fatherland, but each of them remains all his life unconsciously attuned to it."[66] Artists enable us to see the uni-verse with different eyes that enable us to perceive the mysterious and ineffable. They have discovered the nostalgia for the lost fatherland, or lost paradise, that draws the soul homeward.

But for Marcel full understanding of the meaning of all these expe-riences does not come until many years later when, on the way to a party hosted by the Guermantes, he unexpectedly has, in quick succession, three "madeleine" experiences. As on the occasion of tasting the madeleine, he is in a dispirited, gloomy, and bored state of mind, more convinced than ever that he has no gift for literature, a conviction that persuades him that it is pointless to abstain from the frivolous pleasures of social life when it seems that he has nothing greater to hope for. If not yet elderly he is certainly no longer young. He realizes that he has become indifferent to beauties in nature that in earlier years enchanted

65 Ibid., 340–41.
66 Ibid., 342.

him and even moved him to ecstatically inarticulate emotional outbursts. But he is not quite as dispirited as he thinks, because he remains powerfully drawn to his own lost fatherland, and his reason for attending the party is not mere dissipation in meaningless pleasures. The misty feudal past that the name Guermantes still evokes for him, as well as his own memories of his Parisian childhood, give him a "longing to go to the Guermantes party as if in going there I must [be] brought nearer to my childhood and to the depths of my memory where my childhood dwelt."[67] His cab takes him to the vicinity of the Champs-Elysées, which revives memories of walks with the family servant Françoise and meetings with his first love Gilberte, so that he finds that he is traversing not just Parisian streets but "a past, gliding, sad and sweet (*glisssant, triste et doux*); a past which was moreover compounded of so many different pasts that it was difficult for me to recognise the cause of my melancholy . . . ."[68] He tries to remember "snapshots" of Venice, but the boredom this elicits merely reinforces his resignation to having no talent for his deepest aspiration: transforming his past ephemeral experiences into art that embodies the eternal. However, as he soon realizes, his lifelong error is in thinking that art attains the eternal with petrified "snapshots" or ideas. True art is not metamorphic rock but fluid lava.

Then out of the blue occurs the *peripateia*, the sudden reversal, which transfigures gloom and death into luminosity and renewed life. In the courtyard of the Guermantes mansion, where he has arrived after the beginning of the musical performance inside, he fortuitously steps on uneven paving stones and immediately experiences the same upsurge of happiness as he had many years before with the madeleine. He eventually is able to recall that this was a repetition of the sensation of standing on two uneven stones in the baptistery of St. Mark's Cathedral in Venice and of all the sensations linked to it. Within a short time he has two more such powerfully evocative memory deflagrations, involving hearing and touch, as a result of which he embarks on a lengthy meditation on time and art while he waits in the Guermantes's library for the music to end.

67 Proust, *Time Regained,* VI: 241.
68 Ibid., 244.

This is a very long meditation of more than seventy pages, which I can only briefly discuss here. One of the first things that Marcel realizes is that we tend, mistakenly, to evaluate life on the basis not of what it really is, but of the mere appearances that we see and visually recall, "images which preserve nothing of life"[69] or of reality. In the "Combray" section of *Swann's Way* Marcel had recalled that as a child he had sought solitude for uninterrupted reading by hiding in a large canvas and wicker chair in the garden, and had then gone on to draw one of the numerous illuminating analogies in the novel: "And then my thoughts, too, formed a similar sort of recess, in the depths of which I felt that I could bury myself and remain invisible even while I looked at what went on outside. When I saw an external object, my consciousness that I was seeing it would remain between me and it, surrounding it with a thin spiritual border that prevented me from ever touching its substance directly."[70] Waiting in the Guermantes library he remembers this realization, adding that "there is never absolute contact between reality and our intelligence."[71] Far from giving him the world, his intentional, thing-reality consciousness—particularly of things that he *sees*—surrounds all things with an impermeable membrane so that they remain in obscurity. Intelligence, with its intentional consciousness that not only knows but is aware that it knows, serves as a barrier between soul and reality. Attaining enduring reality requires a different consciousness, an entry through a sense other than sight and a faculty other than intelligence into a more pristine non-self-reflective but blissful awareness, an intuition in which we know reality immediately and interiorly. Bergson called this faculty of knowing reality "intuition," and the reality intuited he considered "the absolute," mentioning that it "has often been identified with the infinite" because it can never be exhaustively analyzed, just as the simple internal perception of the motion of raising one's arm cannot be completely reduced by an external observer to motion through a finite number of points because the number of points is potentially infinite. "Now, that which lends itself at the same time both to an indivisible apprehension and to an

69 Ibid., 260.
70 Proust, *Swann's Way,* I: 115.
71 Proust, *Time Regained,* VI: 420.

inexhaustible enumeration is, by the very definition of the word, an infinite."[72]

For Marcel, the effect of this spontaneous eruption of the seemingly forgotten past into the present is that "the past was made to encroach upon the present and I was made to doubt whether I was in the one or the other" because in some way these impressions were extra-temporal (*extra-temporel*), and the inner self that experienced them could emerge from obscurity only when "it could exist and enjoy the essence of things, that is to say: outside time."[73] Only this inner being could enable him to "rediscover days that were long past, the Time that was Lost."[74] He can regain lost time only by transcending time, by contemplating eternity in "fragments of existence withdrawn from Time." This reawakening in him of a "veritable moment of the past" gives him, however fleetingly, reality, "something whose value was eternal" (*une valeur d'éternité*),[75] and thereby restores his appetite for life.

He has found the more essential and vital "existence" that his imagination lacked, which enabled his being, which "is nourished only by the essence of things," "to secure, to isolate, to immobilise—for a moment as brief as a flash of lightning—what normally it never apprehends: a fragment of time in the pure state" (*un peu de temps à l'état pur*).[76] Bergson had consistently identified "immobilizing" with the analytic intellect that creates the false but useful phenomenal world, but Marcel's meditation tells him that we cannot apprehend *truly* permanent reality or essences in the sensuous present, or the intellectualized past, or an intentionally imagined future, but only by a rebirth through an involuntary repetition of a sound, a taste, a texture, a physical position, or an odor previously perceived, which immediately liberates "the permanent and habitually concealed essence of things" and sustains and delights "our true self . . . as it receives the celestial nourishment that is brought to

72 Bergson, *An Introduction to Metaphysics,* 23. The possibly infinite number of points in the motion of raising one's arm is clearly a reference to Zeno's famous paradox.
73 Proust, *Time Regained*, VI: 262.
74 Ibid., 263.
75 Ibid., 513.
76 Ibid., 264.

it."[77] Such an escape from the normal experience of time in which only the present moment seems real, with the past dead and gone forever, like pressed leaves that can be preserved only in desiccated form, creates in Marcel the longed-for, joyous recognition of a permanent reality beyond death and the fear of death, a reality that cannot be lost in time because nothing is truly lost in time. Thus, although our intellect cannot reach reality, there are graced moments in which the "permanent and habitually concealed essences of things" reveal themselves to our sensibilities and memories and, by doing so, make us—however briefly—joyously free from the relentless losses in time. "Fragments of existence withdrawn from Time: these then were perhaps what the being three times, four times brought back to life within me had just now tasted, but the contemplation, though it was of eternity, had been fugitive."[78] Yet he realizes that this fleeting contemplation of the essences of things has been "the only genuine and fruitful pleasure" he has known, and he wonders if this "extra-temporal joy," and not the pleasures of love, was the real allurement in Vinteuil's little phrase for Swann as well as the presentiment of happiness that Marcel himself had heard in the "mysterious, rubescent call" of the septet.[79] He recalls his childhood efforts to contemplate various particular things—"a cloud, a triangle, a church spire, a flower, a stone"—in the hope of penetrating, by a determined effort, to the hidden reality beneath. Now he realizes that intellectual truths are less profound and necessary than "those which life communicates to us against our will in an impression which is material because it enters through the senses but yet has a spiritual meaning which it is possible for us to extract"[80]—including by means of appreciating or creating a work of art in which truth is allowed to emerge from obscurity.

As he continues to reflect in the Guermantes's library, he realizes that simply attempting to repeat experiences, for example by returning to Balbec, will not give him the essences of things or his true self. "Experience had taught me only too well the impossibility of attaining in the real world

77 Ibid.
78 Ibid., 268.
79 Ibid., 272.
80 Ibid., 273.

to what lay deep within myself; I knew that Lost Time (*le Temps perdu*) was not to be found again on the piazza of St. Mark's . . . ."[81] "Lost Time," which exists only in memory, in spirit, cannot be regained by an act of will. He decides that the only way to savor more fully the impressions he wants to make permanent would be "to try to get to know them more completely in the medium in which they existed, that is to say within myself, to try to make them translucid even to their very depths."[82]

These thoughts bring Marcel to a consideration of the true nature and possibilities of art. From his reflections, he concludes that a work of art actually "pre-exists us," and is discovered rather than humanly crafted. It is "the discovery of our true life," of a reality that is so different from our superficial and false beliefs that when perchance we are gifted with "an authentic memory" of its truth it fills us with "an immense happiness."[83] The expression of such an authentic memory in a work of art requires the eschewal of embedding theories in it which would serve only to debase the essence of the art. "A work in which there are theories is like an object which still has its price-tag on it."[84] While absent-mindedly taking first editions from the shelves in the Guermantes library he discovers a copy of *François Le Champi*, and is immediately filled with strong emotion because the book reminds him of his childhood and his child-self, of the night when his mother had read it to him until the early hours of the morning, of all his impressions, emotions, and experiences at the time, and of a thousand trifling, forgotten details of Combray. In short, he finds that Sand's book "contains" the essence of the novel as a work of art because it is able to evoke and preserve a host of memory associations of his inner self. Nothing, he realizes, is truly lost for the luminous consciousness that is a participant in reality—for "a name read long ago in a book contains within its syllables the strong wind and brilliant sunshine that prevailed while we were reading,"[85] and reading it again brings all this back in memory.

81 Ibid., 270.
82 Ibid., 271.
83 Ibid., 277.
84 Ibid., 278.
85 Ibid., 284.

Reality exists hidden beneath the surface appearances which almost always occupy our visual memories and our intellects. Such appearances are, Marcel says, the stuff of tedious pseudo-art, not true art, which finds its questions only because of the mental labor of divesting ourselves of the armor of the intellect:

> We have to rediscover, to reapprehend, to make ourselves fully aware of that reality, remote from our daily preoccupations, from which we separate ourselves by an even greater gulf as the conventional knowledge which we substitute for it grows thicker and more impermeable, that reality which it is very easy for us to die without ever having known and which is, quite simply, our life.[86]

This means that, for Marcel, "real life . . . is literature," and, conversely, literature is real life—not in the sense that literature provides an exact factual account, but in the sense that it enables us to penetrate the shell of conventional knowledge by which our intellect organizes our world and to discern the inner, vital, flowing essence in which the unique past of an individual is contained in every moment of the present. This "real life" exists in everyone but most people never know it because "they do not seek to shed light upon it,"[87] and are content to live in the shallows of intentional consciousness. Real life, expressed in art, constitutes a different world for each original artist who struggles to discern the underlying reality beyond phenomenal experience, and art itself is an expression of individuality.[88] Our intellects, our powers of abstraction, and our ingrained habits of thought lead us astray and must be revitalized by art. Yet our intellect is required to shed the light that brings out "the lineaments" of one's feelings. And suffering is necessary to make reality visible, because it liberates consciousness from the encrustations of habit and conventional knowledge. "The happy years are the lost, the wasted years, one must wait for suffering before one can work," which means that "suffering is the best thing that

86 Ibid., 298.
87 Ibid., 298–99.
88 Ibid., 299.

one can hope to encounter in life."[89] Although it is the happy years that constitute the lost paradise, without suffering, paradise lost could never be regained. It is suffering that instigates the labor necessary to give birth to a work of art. The reality expressed by this memory is not found in the appearances, but only at a depth where appearances have little if any import. Marcel further concludes that since reality discloses itself uniquely in each person's conscious experiences, which are inadequately expressed in each person's verbal responses, the work of a great artist is to translate "the only true book" that "exists already in each one of us."[90] Accordingly, his readers would actually be "the readers of their own selves," with the book serving merely as a kind of magnifying glass which would furnish them with "the means of reading what lay inside themselves."[91]

What all this means, he decides, is that he has been surrounded by people and places that were symbols—"Guermantes, Albertine, Gilberte, Saint-Loup, Balbec, etc."[92]—to which he must restore the meaning obscured by habit by reconstituting life through art. "Indeed the whole art of living is to make use of the individuals through whom we suffer as a step enabling us to draw nearer to the divine form which they reflect and thus joyously to people our life with divinities."[93] He realizes that his own past life, with all of its experiences, far from being wasted as he had thought, had actually provided him with the raw material for a work of literature, like the albumen in the germ-cell of a plant.[94] Since, as Bergson said, the inner life cannot be represented by concepts or even by images, Marcel concludes that it can be represented only by the literary art.

Having, at last, found his subject in his discovery of *l'homme éternel* within himself, he finally enters the Guermantes drawing room where he encounters aged human beings whom he scarcely recognizes after being away for so many years. They appear transmogrified, "puppets which exteriorized Time,"[95] people soon to be engulfed by death. He has

89   Ibid., 319.
90   Ibid., 291.
91   Ibid., 508.
92   Ibid., 302.
93   Ibid., 304.
94   Ibid., 305.
95   Ibid., 342.

become acutely aware of inevitable death, and whereas before his moments of insight he was indifferent to it, he now begins to feel seriously threatened by mortality because it has the power to prevent the coming-to-be of the life-affirming work of art that he is at long last able to create. The possibility of death gives his work an urgency that brooks no more postponements. Now he can finally tell the tale of how, seeking Lost Time, he found that it lay "deep within" himself, it was his "true life,"[96] the enduring "I," the hidden true reality outside time, a paradise he had lost behind the thickening accretions of conventional knowledge. The work of art, the struggle to experience beneath words, matter, and experience something that is different from them, begins from the involuntary moment of awakening; but then will have to "emerge" from himself, in order to share his unique vision with the world:

> Through art alone are we able to emerge from ourselves, to know what another person sees of a universe which is not the same as our own and of which, without art, the landscapes would remain as unknown to us as those that may exist on the moon. Thanks to art, instead of seeing one world only, our own, we see that world multiply itself and we have at our disposal as many worlds as there are original artists . . . worlds which . . . send us still each one its special radiance.[97]

Marcel intends to use art to accomplish what Bergson saw as the purpose of philosophy, *"to invert the habitual direction of the work of thought,"*[98] by intuiting the inward life in the enduring reality of things and self.[99] He sees the work of the artist as "exactly the reverse" of human beings' everyday customs of thinking, which bury

96 Ibid., 270, 277.
97 Ibid., 299.
98 Bergson, *An Introduction to Metaphysics,* 52. Italics in the original.
99 I think T. John Jamieson is correct in his assessment that "Proust manifests an utterly un-Bergsonian anxiety in his essentialism, his Platonic-Augustinian recoil from the Real of Becoming and his desire for fixity in the knowable essences within experience." T. John Jamieson, "From Symbolism to Consciousness via Proust," in *Modern Age* (Summer 2003), 223.

and conceal our true impressions beneath "a whole heap of verbal concepts and practical goals which we falsely call life."[100] The work of art must return us to the beginning, and anamnetically uncover "what has really existed" and "lies unknown within us." His subject is the quest for "eternal" truth, but with an acute awareness of the appearances that usually obscure it. He seeks the reality beneath or behind the appearances, a reality knowable by consciousness and not merely by the senses, although the senses serve to stimulate the search, or the recollection. Realizing that he erred in assuming that he could penetrate through the appearances to the essence of external objects through the efforts of his mind, since their essences or realities can be found only in the graced moments that reveal the mysterious depths of personal consciousness that participates with things in the truth of the whole, Marcel concludes that he has to transcend and abandon his intellect and rely on the rich and complex associations of his own sense memory in order to find reality, to illumine "within the confines of a book" the life "that we live in half-darkness," and to restore "to its true pristine shape" this life "that at every moment we distort."[101] Now that he sees that life is worth living, he has finally begun the work of art.

This leaves us with three questions: Is the first sentence of this essay true? How is the Marcel of the eruptions of memories at the end related to the Marcel at the beginning of the novel? And finally, does Marcel actually attain the insight into reality he desires?

Regarding the first question—whether Marcel produced a work of profound, even limitless, philosophical significance—the answer seems to depend on what is meant by "philosophical significance." If it means what he presumably intended as expressed in *Swann's Way*, a novel to which he would impart profound philosophical meaning, then he did not produce such a work, because the novel is not the story of how his intellect gave meaning to experience. It should be noted that in the later volumes Marcel mentions some articles that he has written, and even one that he has published, but he tells us next to nothing about them,

100 Proust, *Time Regained,* VI: 299–300.
101 Ibid., 507.

presumably because they are not works of art but unsatisfying works of his intellect.

On the other hand, if "philosophical significance" means the quest for and eventual reception of a truth beyond the grasp of the intellect, then it does indeed have profound philosophical significance, not imparted to it by Marcel but imparted *to* Marcel, and to the reader, by the reality in which we participate. Indeed, the realization that the meaning of an individual existence is found in its participation in a greater, "timeless" reality is the central luminous insight. The novel is the tale of how it is a "pre-existent" work of art that was revealed to him—beginning, middle, and end—in a moment when his relaxed and open mind had surrendered all willful efforts to penetrate reality.

Given everything that Marcel says about art and memory, the answer to the second question seems to be that the beginning of the novel is determined by the end, by his discovery of truth and reality in his memories and his awakening to a deeper level of consciousness. Therefore the beginning is about his experience of, and the relationships between different levels of, consciousness, in the midst of which he begins to recover childhood memories, not so much by intense effort as by allowing them to appear in his semi-awake relaxed mind. The description of falling asleep tells the reader that these are memories that have come back to him, almost of their own accord, not memories that he has hunted down. It is the relaxation of the mind and will that is essential for receptivity to truth.

But has he received Truth? Although Marcel refers to the "eternal," and occasionally to the "Beyond," for all of his joy and wonderment at the end he still seems very much time-bound, invoking the immanent and enduring rather than the transcendent and timeless. His impressions are "extra-temporal" because "they had in them something that was common to a day long past and to the present,"[102] not because they are entirely beyond time. His own being is extra-temporal because it does not exist only in a present moment completely isolated from a lost past, but contains and continues his past through the present. Marcel finds his happiness in the realization that the past is not lost or dead but endures

102 Ibid., 262.

richly in the present, that time is *retrouvé* in his memory, and he says that his readers can make the same discovery.[103]

However, the lost paradise for which his soul aches is located in moments in his past, mainly in childhood, and those moments might be experienced as overflowing with happiness only in retrospect. Was Marcel actually overwhelmed with happiness at the moment when, as a young child, he first tasted the tea-soaked madeleine given to him by his invalid aunt, or is the happiness only an artifact of his memory that makes a forgotten moment of the past vividly present, so that, in T. S. Eliot's words, it reveals "the intersection of the timeless moment,"[104] and thereby the presence in every moment of a Presence greater than time? What is the mysterious longing, the nostalgia, so frequently awakened in Swann and Marcel by the "little phrase" of the Vinteuil sonata? Is it not the yearning for a total fulfillment that cannot be found in time at all?

As a work of timeless literature, *À la recherche du temps perdu* is written as a kind of dialogue with the reader, who will be moved (it is hoped) to conduct a similar inquiry himself. The quest is not so much for remembering past experiences as it is for attaining the luminous consciousness in which enduring truth and reality are made visible to the psyche through the kaleidoscopic screen of our habitual experience and analytic thinking. Proust was too much the secular modern man to present this quest in the language of religious faith, transcendence, or God, but he was too spiritually sensitive not to be engaged in preserving the life of the spirit through the search for a reality not completely time-bound, a reality that we do not control, however hard we try, but that erupts into our awareness at times not of our choosing to awaken us from darkness and draw us beyond our false "cave" experiences out into the

103 With this verb, as is common in translations, overtones are lost. The verb *retrouver* does mean "regain" but, according to Cassell's French-English dictionary, also "to find again, to recover, to recognize, and to meet again." Also I cannot help wondering if Proust had in mind the meanings of the reflexive form of the verb (*se retrouver*): "to find each other again; to find oneself again; to be oneself again; to find one's way again; to be met with again."

104 T. S. Eliot, *Four Quartets* (New York: Harcourt, Brace & World, Inc., 1971), 51. The words are from *Little Gidding* I, 51.

sunlit consciousness of a timeless reality that is the only source of true happiness.[105] It is actually not a paradise lost in the past for which Marcel was searching, but transcendence. The discovery that our past is actually not lost but contained in our present selves provides us with a certain sense of meaning and identity as individuals, but seems somewhat inadequate for fulfilling what Kierkegaard called our "eternal consciousness." The moments of the upsurge of memory are experiences of consciousness as luminous rather than intentional, but Marcel thinks that such consciousness is about memories that enable us to rise above time simply because the past is preserved rather than effaced; he doesn't quite see that *l'homme éternel* is not just a complex of memories and associations preserved in our individual psyches, but also a consciousness made luminous by participation in a Reality that entirely transcends our time-bound world. The almost addictive nostalgia evoked in Swann and Marcel by the beauty of the Vinteuil sonata is the innate response to a call from, not merely the composer's fatherland, but the eternal fatherland of every human soul.

105 Jamieson points out that "Voegelin appears to have read all the great French writers of the symbolist movement, seeking in literature a place where the life of the spirit continued to flourish when ideology and positivistic social science drove it out of other cultural fields." "From Symbolism to Consciousness via Proust," 219.

Unsought Revelations of Eternal Reality in Eliot's *Four Quartets* and Proust's *In Search of Lost Time*

Glenn Hughes

T. S. Eliot and Marcel Proust, roughly contemporary literary modernists and two of the most exalted writers of the twentieth century, are rarely compared directly with each other—understandably, given the differences between their stylistic genres and ambitions, their principal themes, and what might be called their ultimate concerns, which for Eliot were religious and for Proust were aesthetic. Still, it is worth examining the fact that the visions of human existence articulated in their mature works share a crucial metaphysical affirmation: each writer takes painstaking care to show that human existence is lived as an "in-between" of time and eternity, participating both in the spatiotemporal world and in a timeless dimension of meaning. Further, both writers also emphasize that the revelations to persons of their participation in timeless reality is always mediated through concrete realities of space and time—that is, human beings can have no *direct* experience of eternal reality: they can apprehend the truth of eternal being only from within the situation of what Eliot calls "the intersection of the timeless with time."

This phrase, from Eliot's poetic masterpiece, *Four Quartets*, distills his understanding of the essence of human existence. And it is this work—a sequence of four poems that summarizes Eliot's mature meditations on personal existence and society, time, history, tradition, language, death, and divinity—that serves as a proper basis for illuminating an important commonality shared by Eliot's portrayal of the "in-between" nature of the human situation and that of Proust as presented in his novel *In Search of Lost Time*: their parallel descriptions of how an everyday sense experience can suddenly and spontaneously become the occasion of an unlooked-for apprehension by consciousness of its participation in eternal being. A comparative look at this element in these works of Eliot and Proust will also reveal, however, important differences in their views—for example, with regard to how we ought to understand and symbolize eternal reality. A few of these differences will be mentioned by way of conclusion; but it is the parallels that are the focus of this essay. And since the clearest way to identify these parallels will be to examine the work of each author in turn, we begin by considering Eliot's presentation in *Four Quartets* of the various modes of human access to awareness of participation in timeless reality, paying special attention to that mode which finds a counterpart in Proust's novel.

Throughout *Four Quartets* Eliot describes or alludes to what he names in its third poem, "The Dry Salvages," as "moments of . . . sudden illumination" (*DS* II, 90–92) in which consciousness is granted an apprehension of the timeless reality that suffuses, grounds, and completes the meaning of all that exists in the order of time.[1] These moments, Eliot indicates, may come upon us as spontaneous, unsought gifts in the midst of daily living; or arise out of purposeful focus in the course of contemplation or prayer; or emerge in the course of deep engagement with works of art. But always they are apprehensions of what Harry Blamires calls "the mystery and the meaning lying beyond the temporal order."[2] They are mystical experiences infused with joy and a brief sense of being released from the limitations and uncertainties of worldly existence, as one feels oneself part of a "beyond" of the world that yet completes the world. In these moments of illumination, as Eliot indicates in the first

1   T. S. Eliot, *Four Quartets* (London: Faber and Faber, 1970), 39. The form of parenthetical reference in the text indicates that the phrase is from section II of "The Dry Salvages," lines 90–92. Hereafter references to each of the four poems, its sections, and pertinent line numbers will be indicated in the same manner using the following abbreviations: *BN* for "Burnt Norton"; *EC* for "East Coker"; *DS* for "The Dry Salvages"; and *LG* for "Little Gidding." All further quotes will be from this edition; page numbers will not be referenced.

2   Harry Blamires, *Word Unheard: A Guide through Eliot's* Four Quartets (London: Methuen & Co. Ltd., 1969), 13–14.

quartet, "Burnt Norton," the world is revealed as sublated within a finalizing fullness of meaning, involving

> *Erhebung* [elevation] without motion, concentration
> Without elimination, both a new world
> And the old made explicit, understood
> In the completion of its partial ecstasy,
> The resolution of its partial horror. (*BN* II, 74–78)

In the illumined grace of these privileged moments, nature and consciousness are revealed to be parts of an ontological unity and wholeness through their involvement in a transcendent reality.

In the opening section of "Burnt Norton" Eliot provides an initial, extended description of such a moment of illumination, one that is unlooked-for and spontaneous, as he describes his visit to a rose garden belonging to the deserted manor-house from which the poem takes its title. In this passage, the mystical moment proper is preceded by experiences of unusual spiritual apprehension: a sense of the presence of "dignified, invisible" personages (perhaps ancestral) and of their "unseen eyebeams" crossing the box-circle of the garden as they gaze upon the roses there; and of "unheard music" to which birds are responding. Then the mystical vision occurs while the poet is looking down into the drained pool at the garden's center:

> Dry the pool, dry concrete, brown edged,
> And the pool was filled with water out of sunlight,
> And the lotos rose quietly, quietly,
> The surface glittered out of heart of light, (*BN* I, 34–37)

Then a cloud passes, the pool is empty again, and while the poet senses a mysterious presence of hidden children and their contained laughter, his vision's vanishing is accompanied by hearing a bird say "Go, go, go," since "human kind / Cannot bear very much reality" (*BN* I, 38–43).

This rose-garden scene, with its accumulating symbols of roses, formal patterns, music, birds, children, ancestors, water, and sunlight, will be evoked by many later phrases and passages in the *Quartets*, and the significance of each symbol will grow throughout the work. But considered in itself, the rose-garden passage performs at the start of the *Quartets* the crucial function of describing in some detail the kind of "moment of illumination" that is unsought, spontaneous, and based on a suddenly charged sense-experience, enabling Eliot later to refer to such moments in an abbreviated way, since their basic character has been established. That character is this: some sense-experience of nature or world has become a charmed medium for the revelation of the mystery of transcendence, and in "an instance of . . . given joy" enabled the poet to experience time united to eternity and his own consciousness as the conjunction of timeless presence and time.[3]

We should note again that *unsought* moments of mystical illumination triggered by suddenly charged sense-experiences are not the only means of access to awareness, of or communion with, eternal reality portrayed by Eliot in the *Quartets*. First, they constitute *only one* of the types of mystical experience that belong to what may be called "the way of light" or "the way of affirmation"; other types include experiences arising from prayer, or by way of engagement with profound works of art. And then also the *Quartets* makes clear that there is an altogether contrasting mode of mystical experience, which may be called "the way of darkness" or "the way of negation," which Eliot alludes to in many passages. Both of these "ways" of intensifying awareness of and attaining a sense of communion with transcendent reality are, of course, described and elaborated at length in both the Eastern and Western mystical traditions; and they are equally emphasized in *Four Quartets*. But it is Eliot's evocations in the *Quartets* of experiences belonging to "the way of light," and *specifically* his references to unlooked-for moments of illumination induced by suddenly-charged sensory experiences, that find striking parallels in Proust's novel. And, notably, it may be argued that this type of moment of illumination has a privileged place in Eliot's portrayal of mystical revelation, because the *Quartets* suggests that these kinds of moment constitute *the most common and elemental way that human beings undergo experiences revealing their participation in the in-between of time and timeless reality*—even if it is the case that, as Eliot points out,

3   Blamires, *Word Unheard*, 13.

these experiences are often, or even typically, "unattended" to, so that their revelatory meaning is "missed" (*DS* II, 93; V, 206).

This privileged status is indicated in part by Eliot's carefully repeated use in the *Quartets* of symbols referring to unsought epiphanies provoked by nature or world. For example, toward the end of "Burnt Norton" Eliot indicates how the sight of a shaft of sunlight has evoked in him a sense of the world's involvement in the timeless—

> Sudden in a shaft of sunlight
> Even while the dust moves
> There rises the hidden laughter
> Of children in the foliage (*BN* V, 169–72)

—both the sunlight ("And the pool was filled with water out of sunlight") and the hidden children's laughter among the leaves referring us back to the moment of illumination in the rose-garden passage in the first movement of the poem.

And the shaft of sunlight returns later, in the last movement of "The Dry Salvages," in what is the "key" or "axial" passage in the *Quartets*, since it most clearly and directly expresses what Eliot wishes to convey about the "in-between" character of the human condition:

> Men's curiosity searches past and future
> And clings to that dimension. But to apprehend
> The point of intersection of the timeless
> With time, is an occupation for the saint—
> No occupation either, but something given
> And taken, in a lifetime's death in love,
> Ardour and selflessness and self-surrender.
> For most of us, there is only the unattended
> Moment, the moment in and out of time,
> The distraction fit, lost in a shaft of sunlight,
> The wild thyme unseen, or the winter lightning
> Or the waterfall, or music heard so deeply
> That it is not heard at all, but you are the music
> While the music lasts. These are only hints and guesses,

Hints followed by guesses; and the rest
Is prayer, observance, discipline, thought and action.
The hint half guessed, the gift half understood, is Incarnation.
Here the impossible union
Of spheres of existence is actual,
Here the past and future
Are conquered, and reconciled, (*DS* V, 199–219)[4]

For most persons, Eliot declares here, the "incarnational" truth about the structure of human existence—that it exists as an intersectional "in-between" of temporal and eternal being—is never clearly grasped or reflected upon. For most, its revelation takes the form only of a distracted "moment" yielding a flashing hint of the mystery of the timeless "beyond" to which proper attention is not given:

For most of us, there is only the unattended
Moment, the moment in and out of time,
The distraction fit, lost in a shaft of sunlight, (*DS* V, 206–08)

The lines also indicate that the image of the shaft of sunlight—which carries with its symbolism, from earlier passages in the *Quartets*, echoes of children, laughter, and garden—is an elemental symbol for Eliot of the experience of timelessness-in-time. It conveys for him how an intense sensory experience of the natural world, in an unlooked-for moment, can

4   The word "Incarnation" in this passage signifies not only the presence of divine fullness in Christ, but also the presence of eternal reality within *all* human consciousness. Elizabeth Drew argues that the symbol of "Incarnation," appearing only this once in the *Quartets*, even more generally refers to the presence and manifestation of eternal being in *all* temporal reality, not just human existence. "Incarnation," she writes, should be understood as "a *principle* active throughout the universe[,] . . . an invisible energy manifesting itself in [all] the phenomena of sense." Elizabeth Drew, *T. S. Eliot: The Design of his Poetry* (New York: Charles Scribner's Sons, 1949), 187. The lines that follow Eliot's introduction of the symbol, however, and continuing to the end of the poem, indicate that his concern in *this* section of "The Dry Salvages" is with the ontological presence of "the intersection of the timeless with time" in human consciousness.

evoke in human consciousness a glimpse of eternal being—though for the large majority of persons, any such moment is experienced only as a passing "distraction fit."

Other recurring symbols of this type appear in the *Quartets*. In the second poem, "East Coker," for example, immediately following the poet's promise that a spiritual attitude of openness can lead to an apprehension of the eternal-in-time, a sequence of sense-experiences is mentioned:

> Whisper of running streams, and winter lightning.
> The wild thyme unseen and the wild strawberry,
> The laughter in the garden . . . (*EC* III, 129–31)

These are clearly allusions to sensory triggers of unlooked-for moments of illumination. And while the "laughter in the garden" directs us back to the rose-garden epiphany, the other images here—as we have just seen—will be echoed in the following quartet, "The Dry Salvages," where the "moment in and out of time" is instantly associated with trigger-experiences of

> . . . a shaft of sunlight,
> The wild thyme unseen, or the winter lightning
> Or the waterfall, (*DS* V, 208–10)

These recurring references to the smell of wild thyme, winter lightning, and the sound of water (whispering or falling), confirm their importance to the poet as sense-experiences occasioning moments of epiphany.

The foregoing does not exhaust the references in the *Quartets* to unlooked-for moments of illumination occasioned by sense-experiences of nature or world, but it will suffice for allowing us to consider certain *characteristics* of these experiences, which, we will find, have a parallel in Proust's descriptions of epiphanies of eternal being in *In Search of Lost Time*.

A first characteristic of this type of mystical experience is its involuntariness. It is unsought and unprepared-for—it comes as an *unexpected* gift. This separates it from the types of moments of illumination that arise from a searching engagement with a work of art, or as the fruit of prayer or meditation. Both of the latter indeed come suddenly and unpredictably, but in their contexts they are also hoped-for, and in a sense anticipated: in such activities the psyche longs for the gift of the visionary moment. By contrast, the moments we have been describing come, so to speak, out of nowhere; they are gifted to the recipient in the most radical sense of the term, arriving when they will to the startled consciousness as a consequence of a sensory experience whose catalytic function could never have been suspected or predicted.

A second characteristic to note is that such experiences are quite idiosyncratic or personal. The rose-garden episode, for example, while rich with symbolic overtones of both a Biblical and more general spiritual character, is clearly intended to be read as autobiographical, describing an experience of Eliot's during his visit to a deserted manor-house in Gloucestershire, and therefore as peculiar to the contingencies pertaining to his unique person and situation. Likewise, in a less elaborated way, references to the aroma of unseen wild thyme, to a flash of winter lightning, to the hidden laughter of children, and to the whisper of a running stream as triggers of mystical experience are clearly personal, even while Eliot the poet obviously intends them to signify all such experiences of nature or world that evoke in a person's consciousness the mystery of a timeless beyond.

A third feature of such experiences is that the *objects* that are their catalysts are trivial—they have no special intrinsic significance. The smell of an herb, an angled beam of sunlight, the sound of children laughing, a compelling strain of music—these are everyday phenomena. But such phenomena can suddenly become filled with transcendent suggestiveness. Through the presence of certain conditions—a happenstance of personal openness and readiness, an accident of timing, unpredictable elements of personal memory and remembered associations—they can become mediators of what the philosopher Bernard Lonergan calls reality's "undefined surplus of significance."[5] This again distinguishes

---

5   Bernard Lonergan, *Insight: A Study of Human Understanding*, eds. Frederick E. Crowe and Robert M. Doran, vol 3. of *Collected Works of Bernard Lonergan* (Toronto: University of Toronto Press, 1992), 556.

such moments of illumination from those that arise from encounters with artworks. The best works of art have been designed, one might say, to evoke such a moment. But the scent of wild thyme, or a drained pool in a formal garden, merely happen, despite their trivial nature, to be occasions of illuminative vision.

A fourth characteristic of such experiences is that they bring a unique joy or happiness with their illumination. They fill the psyche for a moment with a sense of ultimate harmony and resolution, a happy sense of the reconciliation of temporal life with the depths of timeless meaning, and this liberates the self, momentarily, from its everyday emotional, intellectual, and existential burdens. In "The Dry Salvages," Eliot makes clear that this is a happiness unlike all other forms of satisfaction or fulfillment, one whose nature is not conveyed by the word "happiness" in any of its normal uses (*DS* II, 90–96). It is an experience that delivers a brief taste of the joy that informs the spiritual promise made by the mystic Julian of Norwich that "All shall be well and / All manner of thing shall be well" (*LG* V, 255–56), a promise that Eliot quotes twice in his final quartet, "Little Gidding."

Finally, such moments allow consciousness to feel itself, as Eliot puts it in "Burnt Norton," "surrounded / By a *grace of sense*" (*BN* II, 72–73; emphasis added)—a phrase that compactly suggests how in such moments the whole of reality perceived by the senses, together with the consciousness doing the sensing, is experienced as imbued with transcendent *value*. The consequence is that, as Helen Gardner writes, "the world of nature is [revealed as] the field of grace"—that is, the entirety of the sensed temporal order is translated into a reality charged with eternal significance.[6] This "grace of sense" is, again, often "unattended" to—that is to say, not noticed for what it is and not reflected upon for what it reveals about existence. But, Eliot indicates in a number of passages in the *Quartets*, we *ought to* reflect upon it. We have a duty, Eliot indicates, both to *remember* the "ecstasy" of the moment of illumination and to *consider in its light* "the agony / Of death and birth" (*EC* III, 131–33), because it is this remembrance and consideration that shows our ex-

6 Helen Gardner, *The Art of T. S. Eliot* (New York: E. P. Dutton & Co., Inc., 1959), 176.

periences of suffering, tedium, and anxiety to be meaningful parts of an encompassing if mysterious pattern through their ontological involvement in eternal meaning. Through remembrance and reflection on such moments, we can—as we should—come to love our existences in the world, and to love the ground of both existence and world, "the ground of our beseeching" (*LG* III, 199). By doing this, Eliot writes in "Little Gidding," we may find freedom from entanglements in all worldly desires and goals, past and future:

> This is the use of memory:
> For liberation—not less of love but expanding
> Of love beyond desire, and so liberation
> From the future as well as the past. (*LG* III, 156–59)

This detailing of five characteristics of unsought moments of illumination raises an interesting question: are these types of moment granted to *everyone*, so that anyone might use attention and memory to acknowledge a mystery of timeless meaning and interpret existence in light of its truth? Eliot implies that this is the case in the already-quoted "Incarnation" passage in "The Dry Salvages," where he makes a distinction between those whom he calls "saints" and the rest of humanity:

> . . . to apprehend
> The point of intersection of the timeless
> With time, is an occupation for the saint—
> No occupation either, but something given
> And taken, in a lifetime's death in love,
> Ardour and selflessness and self-surrender.
> For most of us, there is only the unattended
> Moment, the moment in and out of time,
> The distraction fit, lost in a shaft of sunlight, (*DS* V, 200–08)

The saint, in other words, is one who structures a *vocation* around attending to conscious human existence being constituted as the intersection of timelessness with time. But all of us who are not saints are not bereft of our own intimations of eternity. Every consciousness is naturally disposed toward, and *typically and normatively* receives its glimpses of, the mystery of transcendent meaning. For any particular person the *significance* of such a glimpsed apprehension may certainly be missed, and in fact usually is missed—sometimes through being willfully rejected. Still, some understanding of that significance exists universally *in potentia* to be accorded its due and to be allowed to inform one's interpretation of existence.

Three last points should be made about Eliot's portrayal of moments of illumination based on unlooked-for, intense sense-experiences. The first is that such moments—as with *all* types of mystical experience—make it clear that we can only understand the true nature of human consciousness by appreciating that it has, to our minds, an inescapably paradoxical structure. This is because one must describe human consciousness as being at all times *both within and beyond time*. Mystical experiences make that ontological status explicit to the experiencing mind. Thus in "Burnt Norton" Eliot writes of mystical moments, both in the rose garden and elsewhere:

> I can only say, *there* we have been: but I cannot say where.
> And I cannot say, how long, for that is to place it in time.
> (*BN* II, 68–69)

And in "Little Gidding," describing his spiritual self-awareness when visiting the religiously significant site of the small village that gives the poem its title:

> Here, the intersection of the timeless moment
> Is England and nowhere. (*LG* I, 52–53)

Finally, the paradox is most clearly announced when Eliot writes of the fact of "Incarnation," referring both to divine presence in the person of Christ and the timeless-in-time manifested in every human consciousness:

> Here the impossible union
> Of spheres of existence is actual, (*DS* V, 216–17)

The second point is that, since such moments of illumination show one's temporal life to be part of a unified pattern grounded in a mystery of timelessness, they enable one to embrace one's existence as *a meaningful and integrated development* rather than as simply a sequence of experiences with transitory meaning ending in the nothingness of death. Of course, if a person remains oblivious or resistant to the eternal, due, perhaps, to certain inclinations of imagination, or to fear of spiritual responsibility, or as a result of the "imaginative oblivion"[7] induced by contemporary visions of reality that are reductively immanentist or materialist—if one's search for meaning, for whatever reason, *only* "searches past and future / And clings to that dimension" (*DS* V, 199–200) and never accedes to consciousness's normative openness to acknowledgement of the dimension of the eternal—then life will seem to have no significant destination (*DS* II, 72); death will replace God as the ultimate measure of reality (*DS* II, 83); and worldly existence will appear to be nothing more than "waste sad time" (*BN* V, 174).

Third and finally, it is possible that a person's insight into the fact that human consciousness participates in eternal being can lead to the idea that our existence in time is irrelevant. Eliot points out that the opposite is the case. What the moments show is that the meaning of existence *is* its pilgrimage through time in conscious relationship to the timeless reality in which it participates, and that we should struggle to dignify our temporal existences through openness and responsiveness to the perfections of eternal being. This fact suggests that the reason Eliot places so much emphasis in the *Quartets* on unlooked-for, sensation-based moments of illumination is because they indicate more obviously and vividly than any other type of mystical experience, first, that timeless being is revealed *only* through the medium of concrete bodily existence and its experiences; and second, that the human apprehension of transcendence occurs *in order to* reveal temporal existence as meaningful, through liberating us from our fear that perishable being is all

7   The phrase is Eric Voegelin's; see Voegelin, *Order and History, Volume V: In Search of Order*, ed. Ellis Sandoz, vol 18. of *The Collected Works of Eric Voegelin* (Columbia, MO: University of Missouri Press, 2000), 76–77.

that human existence is. A passage from "Burnt Norton" sums up these points with clarity and beauty:

> To be conscious is not to be in time
> But only in time can the moment in the rose-garden,
> The moment in the arbour where the rain beat,
> The moment in the draughty church at smokefall
> Be remembered; involved with past and future.
> Only through time time is conquered. (*BN* II, 85–90)

Our "conquering" of time is not escape from it; it is overcoming the oppressive and anxiety-inducing delusion that the temporal world is the only reality, that finitude and mortality are the ultimate measure of meaning. The illumination of timelessness is thus, crucially, the illumination of *time's* significance—an illumination that can allow us to consciously embrace, and thus *redeem*, the time past and time future of our existences through existentially accepting their ontological integration with the mystery of eternal meaning.

Let us turn, now, to selected passages and themes in Proust's vast novel *In Search of Lost Time* to examine how Proust describes, in a fashion remarkably similar to Eliot in *Four Quartets*, sensory experiences of natural or worldly phenomena that, in a sudden and unsought-for manner, provide occasions for a self to recognize its participation in eternal reality.

Proust's great work is most well-known for exploring in extraordinarily nuanced detail the "interiority" of a man's consciousness during important episodes in the course of his life—the life of the narrator, "Marcel," who closely resembles but is not identical to the author Marcel Proust. The beauties of its innovative, long-winded style always serve the novel's purpose of expressing, with a perspicuity and subtlety unprecedented in fiction, the inner world of a character's experiences, reflections, insights, memories, feelings, and judgments; and therefore it is as a *psychological* novel, exhaustively rich in self-analysis and detailed, self-revealing aperçus, that Proust's masterpiece is principally described and appreciated. It is less remarked-upon that the novel's most famous theme—its account of "involuntary memory" as a key to profound self-discovery—provides Proust with the psychological basis for presenting a *metaphysical* vision of self and world that allows the narrator Marcel at last to understand, toward the end of the seven-volume story, that his life as a whole has not been meaningless. Finishing the novel, one realizes that its narrative coherence depends above all on it being the story of Marcel's regular intimations, and finally his explicit discovery, of the truth that human existence participates in eternal reality. The central thematic climax of this long story turns out to be the importance to Marcel of the revelation that the most important experiences of his life have all been signs and invitations summoning him to explicitly realize, through careful reflection, that there is a transcendent reality in which, in some mysterious way, his conscious being has always participated.

So while Proust is widely recognized as a psychologist of astonishing insight, it is also true—though it scarcely factors in his public image—that he is one of the most important mystics in twentieth-century literature. It is the narrator's mystical experiences that both integrate the novel's story and, in the end, allow Marcel to make sense of his life as a whole. And of particular importance for our analysis, the most emphasized of Marcel's mystical experiences are those in which a seemingly trivial sense-experience suddenly and unexpectedly triggers a joyful, transformational awareness that the self participates in a reality beyond time and world.

But here we should pause to ask: do these mystical experiences, which belong to the fictional Marcel of the novel, reflect Proust's own experiences? The question may be confidently answered in the affirmative, because it is possible to find in Proust's letters and essays statements and descriptions that correspond to Marcel's expositions of mystical experiences and affirmations of eternal reality. As with Eliot in *Four Quartets*, in Proust's novel the most profound of the author's personal experiences provide core materials for the creation of an artwork meant to communicate to readers the character of those experiences, which for both authors have a more-than-personal relevance since they are offered as antidotes to modern visions of existence that reduce the meaning of human life to the transience and perishability of its temporal conditions.

In Proust's novel, Marcel's mystical experiences are presented most fully in episodes describing "epiphanies" undergone by him, referred to in the novel's final volume, *Time Regained*, in a general or summary way as *impressions bienheureuses*.[8] These are ecstatic moments in which he suddenly and unexpectedly feels himself existing simultaneously both in and outside of time. The most well-known of these is the moment early in the novel in which Marcel, as an adult, tasting crumbs of a madeleine in a spoonful of tea, is suddenly flooded with a vivid sense of reliving certain experiences of his childhood, a *perfect* reliving that could only be possible, Marcel concludes, because his consciousness and its memories belong not only to time but to an imperishable, timeless reality.[9]

As described in Proust's novel, there are three sources of *impressions bienheureuses*. The least important, as he presents it, involves a considered contemplation of natural or human-made objects. A second is experiences of profound engagement with works of art. But the third, and most important, source is sensations, trivial in themselves, that suddenly induce experiences of "involuntary memory" such as the experience arising from tasting the tea-soaked crumbs of madeleine.

This is the type of mystical experience in Proust's novel that, in his portrayal of it, closely echoes the type we have focused upon in *Four Quartets*. What occurs in the episodes of involuntary memory, as we have noted with respect to the madeleine episode, is that a sensory experience in the lived present brings suddenly into Marcel's consciousness a similar sensory experience from his past life, but in a manner that is uncanny because the past sensation, and its lived context, is not experienced as "past" but as overwhelmingly and vividly *present*. As Marcel says of one such experience: "I now recaptured the *living reality* in a *complete* and involuntary recollection"; and of another, "it was not only an echo, a duplicate of a past sensation that I was made to feel . . . it *was that past sensation itself.*" His self has suddenly become, simultaneously, "the self that originally lived" the past sensation while yet remaining the self living and experiencing the present analogous sensation.[10] And in

8   Proust, *Time Regained*, VI: 262 ("happy impressions").
9   Proust, *Swann's Way*, I: 60–64.
10 Proust, *Sodom and Gomorrah*, IV: 211, 212; *Time Regained*, VI: 267 (emphasis added).

this "magnetism of an identical moment," as he puts it, the self is not just aware of, but *is* the self of both "times."[11]

What gives Proust the confidence, in philosophical terms, to make such an assertion? His explanation has a Platonic ring to it. Marcel comes to the conclusion that a present sensation can simultaneously make *fully and truly present to consciousness* a similar past sensation because the two sensations share a common timeless "essence"—and in such a moment, Marcel has suddenly and involuntarily attained access to this essence.[12] But this attainment that enables the self to "enjoy the essence[s] of things" can only be possible if there is a dimension of the self that is itself "extra-temporal." As Marcel relates in the novel, the *impressions bienheureuses* of involuntary memory lead him to judge that in such moments the conscious self is in fact "liberated from the contingencies of time," that it briefly and miraculously escapes from the world of perishability.[13] Consequently Marcel/Proust is unequivocal on the fact that there is an eternal reality and that humans can know of their participation in it; that there as "a portion of our mind more durable" than the temporal self; and that he has tasted the "contemplation . . . of eternity."[14]

Of course time is very much alive in the *impressions bienheureuses* of involuntary memory, even as the self "escapes from time," because the moments involve time-bound sensations. They are thus experiences of being simultaneously in time and outside time—or, in Eliot's words, experiences of "the intersection of the timeless with time." So, just as in *Four Quartets*, epiphanies of transcendence evoked by suddenly transportive sensations allow the self to recognize the time past, time present, and time future of one's existence as meaningful through their participation in the imperishable meaning of eternal being.

Examining more closely Proust's epiphanies arising from involuntary memory, we can see that they share precisely the same five characteristics that we identified as belonging to the unsought "moments of illumination" in *Four Quartets*.

11 Proust, *Swann's Way*, I: 62.
12 Proust, *Time Regained*, VI: 253–59, 262.
13 Ibid., 262–63, 290.
14 Ibid., 301, 268.

First, as already conveyed by the phrase "involuntary memory," Proust emphasizes that the mystical experiences induced by sense-experiences are unsought and unexpected—"chance happening[s]" that take the narrator by surprise. Marcel goes so far as to state, in his extended reflection on their nature and meaning in the last volume of the novel, that "their *essential character* was that I was not free to choose them, that such as they were they were given to me"; while at the same time he makes a point of asserting that no other truths are more important to a person than those that "life communicates to us against our will in an impression which is material because it enters us through the senses but yet has a spiritual meaning which it is possible for us to extract."[15] As with Eliot's portrayal of similar mystical experiences in *Four Quartets*, we find that this characteristic of involuntariness and chance is what most clearly distinguishes these "moments of illumination" from those that arise through encounters with great works of art. These are unsought moments, and might even come "against our will."

Second, each such *impression bienheureuse* is presented as arising from an experiential trigger that is pointedly personal, peculiar to Marcel's biography, character, disposition, and situation. Tasting bits of a madeleine in a spoonful of tea causes an epiphany in Marcel for wholly idiosyncratic reasons, and the same is true for each epiphany in the novel: the mystical moments resulting from touching the top button of his boot as he begins undressing in the seaside hotel in Balbec, or from standing on uneven paving-stones in the courtyard of the Guermantes mansion in Paris, or from hearing the harsh noise of water in a pipe in the mansion's waiting-room.[16] Whether or not Proust in these passages is describing actual sensory experiences from his own life that evoked apprehensions of timelessness, their purely personal character is obvious.

Third, the objects involved in these *impressions bienheureuses* are not important in themselves; they become charged with significance by the chance of their being momentarily the medium for an apprehension

15 Ibid., 256, 274, 273 (emphasis added).
16 Proust, *Sodom and Gomorrah*, IV: 210–15; *Time Regained*, VI: 253–56; 266–67.

of transcendence. Marcel explicitly reflects on this fact, remarking that *"however trivial its material may seem to be,"* the mind will be led to value a particular sensation or "impression" as the vehicle of an epiphany and a great joy.[17] This triviality of the sense-objects that trigger such mystical experiences is especially notable in the narrator's account of his childhood intimations of eternity in the first volume of the novel, *Swann's Way*. There Marcel describes how, as a child, he would sense some "mystery that lay hidden in a shape or a perfume . . . the play of sunlight on a stone, a roof, the sound of a bell, the smell of fallen leaves"—inklings of a wondrous unknown that only later in life would he understand to be eternal and essential reality.[18] Such images compare readily with the wild thyme unseen, the whisper of a running stream, and the winter lightning of *Four Quartets*.

Fourth, Marcel's *impressions bienheureuses* typically bring him a unique kind of joy, and he repeatedly emphasizes its distinctive quality, calling it variously an "exquisite pleasure," an "all-powerful joy," an "unreasoning pleasure," a "positive rapture," a "special pleasure."[19] And because it entails his sense of participating in eternity, he goes so far as to describe it as an "extra-temporal joy" and even a "supraterrestrial joy."[20]

Fifth and finally, as in Eliot's account in the *Quartets* of similar moments, the *impressions bienheureuses* bring with them a feeling of liberation from being bound to the limitations and contingencies of temporal existence. Thus, as Harold March points out, the *impressions* that guide Marcel to eternity lead him also to *freedom*, as all of his anxieties involving worldly existence fall away and even death becomes "a matter of indifference."[21] For example, in the most well-known *impression bienheureuse,* Marcel recollects how, upon tasting the tea-soaked crumbs of madeleine, "at once the vicissitudes of life had become indifferent to me, its disasters

---

17 Proust, *Time Regained*, VI: 275 (emphasis added).
18 Proust, *Swann's Way*, I: 253.
19 Ibid., 60, 61, 251–52; *Within a Budding Grove*, II: 91.
20 Proust, *Time Regained*, VI: 272; *The Captive*, V: 347.
21 Proust, *Time Regained*, VI: 257. Harold March, *The Two Worlds of Marcel Proust* (New York: A. S. Barnes & Company, Inc., Perpetua Edition, 1961), 195.

innocuous, its brevity illusory . . . I had ceased now to feel mediocre, contingent, mortal." And of the special pleasure accompanying this sudden freedom from temporality with all its concerns, Marcel asks: "Whence could it have come to me, this all-powerful joy?"[22] The "whence" is eventually discovered by Marcel to be "eternal reality," as recounted in the last volume of the novel, where he insists—as does Eliot in the *Quartets*—on the importance of the use of *voluntary* memory to return attention to, and carefully reflect upon, the metaphysical significance of his epiphanies. And again like Eliot, Proust envisions the ultimate purpose of this gift of freedom, and joy, to be the expansion of love—in Proust's phrasing, the "restoring" of our love from its normal restricted objects to "its generality," so that we may give our love "to all, to the universal spirit."[23] Despite the fact that Marcel in the novel indicates scarce capacity to exhibit such growth, Marcel's/Proust's declarations here clearly echo Eliot's remark that the essential "use of memory" is the expansion of love.

Having established five shared characteristics between Eliot's unsought moments of illumination and Proust's *impressions bienheureuses* arising from involuntary memory, we may ask the same question about these epiphanies of Proust that we asked about Eliot's unsought "moments": namely, are such experiences available to *everyone*? Proust's answer, it seems, is the same as Eliot's: knowledge of eternal reality, Marcel says, is "all the time immanent in [all] men," but, he adds, it is "very easy for us to die without having known" its truth. The narrator of *In Search of Lost Time* has no doubt that every person has "moments of perception" that constitute glimpses of transcendence which, if understood, would reveal that "life [is] worth living"; but relatively few persons pay close enough attention, or use memory and reflection, to search out their meaning.[24]

Three final remarks complete our study of the parallels between Proust's and Eliot's portrayals of mystical experiences.

First of all, Proust, like Eliot, recognizes that a proper understanding of human consciousness entails acknowledging that it has, to our finite

22 Proust, *Swann's Way*, I: 60.
23 Proust, *Time Regained*, VI: 301.
24 Ibid., 298, 507.

minds, an essentially paradoxical structure, since it exists at every moment both within a spatiotemporal locatedness of "here" and "now" and in some "beyond" of the world, in a dimension of transcendence that can only be indicated negatively (as Eliot does in the *Quartets*) as a "nowhere" or a "never" or an "always." Marcel/Proust underlines this paradox when he describes how the *impressions bienheureuses* induced by "involuntary memory" involve his experiencing a past sensation as belonging to the past, and thus as "annihilated," but at the very same moment as fully ontologically present in his consciousness, and thus as "surviving" in that dimension of his consciousness that somehow has a mysterious "extra-temporal being."[25] This strange "contradiction of survival and annihilation," as Marcel puts it, this paradoxical "synthesis of [the] survival and annihilation" of time, is only explicable on the assumption, first, that there is an eternal reality that bisects time, and second, that human consciousness itself is the locus where awareness of the temporal world and awareness of timeless reality intersect.[26] And since each conscious existence is truly a *union* of time and eternity, there can be no experience of eternity "in itself"; it is only experienced within the paradoxical intersection of time and timelessness, in the incarnate consciousness where "the impossible union / Of spheres of existence is actual" (*DS* V, 216–17).

Second, the *impressions bienheureuses* reveal to Marcel that his existence in the temporal world constitutes a unified and meaningful *story*, rather than being just a congeries of disconnected chronological episodes. As Marcel states at one point, the "impressions" that had given rise in him to apprehensions of eternal reality, which he had experienced "at remote intervals" during the course of his life, at last were able to become, when he understood their significance, "foundation-stones for the construction of a *true* life"—that is, a life that through reconstitutive memory has become "true" because it can now be seen to add up to an ontologically integrated story by virtue of its continual participation in eternal reality.[27] The discovery and appropriation of this truth is

25 Proust, *Time Regained*, VI: 262.
26 Proust, *Sodom and Gomorrah*, IV: 215, 216.
27 Proust, *The Captive*, V: 347 (emphasis added).

enormously important for Marcel, because it at last dispels his suspicion—a suspicion that haunts him throughout the novel, and grows especially burdensome during the stages of life described in the fourth, fifth, and sixth volumes of the novel—that his existence in time is no more significant than a perishable dream.

Thus thirdly, Proust emphasizes in his novel, as Eliot does in *Four Quartets*, that the revelation of eternity does not negate the significance of temporal existence, but rather irradiates it with enduring meaning. Marcel's recognition of this truth is the narrative climax of the novel, since its entire story unfolds as Marcel's search for the "lost time" of his childhood, youth, and middle age in order to find its meaningfulness, which he discovers through realizing that it participates in the reality of eternal being. Thus by the end of the novel, Marcel is "[r]econciled to time and to his own place both in and outside it."[28] His mystical experiences have allowed him to understand his own existence in the world as neither a continual loss of existential investment nor a series of experiential episodes ending in waste and disappointment, but as truly "regained," or redeemed.

To summarize: both Eliot in the *Quartets* and Proust in his novel are concerned not only with presenting human consciousness as "the intersection of the timeless with time," but with portraying spontaneous, unlooked-for moments of sensory encounter with objects in the world as occasions of mystical experience, or epiphany, in which persons undergo illuminative, revelatory awareness of their participation in timeless reality. They further present *this* type of mystical experience as *potentially available to everyone*—if they are attended to, remembered, and properly reflected upon. If these conditions are met, Eliot and Proust agree, they secure for a person assurance that his or her existence in time is meaningful, and that it has a genuine biographical coherence or unity, because it ontologically participates at all times in a timeless ground of meaning.

Finally, one other major point of agreement between Eliot and Proust regarding mystical experiences that we have only glancingly referred to in our look at each author should be emphasized: for both writers

28   Shattuck, *Proust's Way*, 45.

"moments of illumination" can be occasioned by engagement with works of art. Eliot makes this clear in various places in *Four Quartets*: in a passage describing a "Chinese jar" that "[m]oves perpetually in its stillness" (*BN* V, 142–43), suggesting how an artwork can convey to a receptive observer the mystery of the intersection of time and timelessness, motion and the transcendent reality beyond motion; in his lines describing "music heard so deeply / That it is not heard at all, but you are the music / While the music lasts" (*DS* V, 210–12), which may refer to an unsought moment of vision, but also suggests experiences of intensely attentive engagement with a musical work; and above all, in the extended passages in three of the four quartets that address the art of writing, and specifically the difficulties and highest aims of poetry. These passages turn the reader's attention to the fact that *Four Quartets* is itself an artwork *whose principal purpose* is to evoke illuminative recognition that human existence is lived in "the intersection of the timeless with time," and to urge the reader to use memory, "prayer, observance, discipline, [and] thought" (*DS* V, 214) to attend to and reflect on the meaning of "moments of illumination."

For Proust, too, art is a crucial medium for inducing mystical recognition of the situatedness of human consciousness in-between time and eternity. In fact, Proust understands this to be the sole *true* purpose of art: for him, as Harold March writes, "[i]t is the function of art" to induce "glimpses of the other world" and also to "develop these insights and to use them for the illumination of life in the world of time."[29] This idea is the subject matter of a number of episodes in Proust's novel, but perhaps is most explicitly expressed in the novel's fifth volume, *The Captive*, in which a Septet Marcel is listening to induces a transportive, mystical awareness of eternal being. Reflecting on this experience, the narrator explains that "[in this art] I had been able to apprehend the strange summons which I should henceforth never cease to hear, as the *promise and proof* that there existed something other" than the temporal world. Later in the volume he declares that it "is inconceivable that a piece of sculpture or a piece of music which gives us [such an experience] does not correspond to some definite spiritual reality," for if such were the case

---

29   March, *The Two Worlds of Marcel Proust*, 246.

"life would be meaningless."[30] That Proust writes extensively about the manners in which art can evoke this sense of mystery is scarcely surprising, since in the novel's climactic passages in its last volume, *Time Regained*, Marcel will find his own vocation in creating a work of literary art—the novel the reader is finishing—whose most important purpose is to show and to explain that mystical epiphanies *do* reveal spiritual reality, and that life is *not* meaningless.

A few words only remain to be said about the differing metaphysical visions of Eliot and Proust, with regard to their understanding and symbolization of eternal reality and of the *meaning* of human participation in eternal being—and why Eliot's ultimate concerns may be properly described as *religious*, while Proust's are better identified as *aesthetic*.

Eliot is a Christian; and the vision of the cosmos, existence, and human destiny in *Four Quartets* is a Christian vision. It is not Christian in a narrowly exclusivist sense; it is a Christian vision that is profoundly ecumenic and universalist. This is well indicated in the range of imagery and symbols used to evoke experiences of transcendence in the *Quartets*. In addition to its reliance on the symbol of Incarnation, its lyrical evocations of the divine persons of Creator, Son, Virgin, and Spirit, and its explicit use of the symbols and sayings of such Christian predecessors as Dante, St. John of the Cross, and Julian of Norwich, the poems of the *Quartets* also draw explicitly from Buddhist, Hindu, and Platonic or Neoplatonist traditions and language, and its evocation of mystical and meditative experiences is clearly intended to suggest a global range of references, making clear that the mystical experiences that concern Eliot are *universally* available. But at the same time, true to Christian understanding, the *Quartets* affirms the timeless ground of being to be transcendent divine love, a being beyond time and desiring, that nonetheless suffers itself to be manifested as desire in the divinely-caused movement of creaturely longing and love:

> Love is itself unmoving,
> Only the cause and end of movement,
> Timeless, and undesiring

---

30   Proust, *The Captive*, V: 350, 504 (emphasis added).

> Except in the aspect of time
> Caught in the form of limitation
> Between un-being and being. (*BN* V, 163–68)

For Eliot, therefore, human consciousness is a created "form of limita-tion" that can participate *knowingly* in transcendent divine love, a worldly site where immanent being is *directly* permeable by the revela-tion of the divine transcendence that, properly understood, is the unre-stricted act of Love that is the Christian God.

This means that, for Eliot, all "moments of illumination"—whether occasioned surprisingly by suddenly-charged sense-experiences, or by a work of art, or by any other catalyst—are "hints and guesses" (*DS* V, 212) meant to guide us to discover that eternal reality is the divine Cre-ator of world and self, and to guide us thereby into a responsive rela-tionship to Him, in a conscious reciprocity of seeking and being drawn. And, importantly, it is this understanding of transcendent reality that ac-counts for Eliot's presentation in the *Quartets* of *both* "ways" of ap-proaching eternal being: the "way of light," to which the "moments of illumination" belong; and the ascetic or apophatic "way of darkness" or "negation." The former, as Harry Blamires emphasizes, is a *"given* way": it is experienced as a gift bestowed. But the latter is a *"chosen* way": it is the way of prayer, of ascetic "[d]essication of the world of sense" (*BN* III, 119), of "descent" into the darkness and stillness of interiority to en-counter the being that is beyond all world and sense, so that the darkness, in Eliot's words in "East Coker," "shall be the darkness of God" (*EC* III, 113).[31]

By contrast, in Proust's portrayal of types of mystical experience, there is no mention of the "way of darkness" or "negation"—of *chosen* practices of seeking communion with the eternal—which is commen-surate with there being no descriptions in the novel of eternal reality as divine Creator, or of Marcel engaging in prayer, or of Marcel feeling himself drawn by divine Love. All of this is consistent with Proust's metaphysics. He never symbolizes transcendence as "God," even though at times he uses adjectives such as "divine" and "supernatural" to refer

---

31 Blamires, *Word Unheard*, 31 (emphasis added).

to what he calls the "essential" reality of eternal being. On one occasion, it is true, Proust refers to a "universal love" of which his perennially disappointed efforts to love another person he "knew" to be a "tiny fragment"; and on another he refers to a "universal spirit" to which, he says, "the portion of [his] mind more durable" than the part of the self that dies should "give [its] love [and] the understanding of this love."[32] But in the voluminous pages of the novel there is no expansion on these unique references to a "universal love" and "universal spirit." In the end Proust's vision of transcendence remains strictly impersonal.

And one result of Proust's view of eternal reality as transcendent impersonal "essences" is his conviction that there can be no higher human duty than to create artworks that might evoke in others mystical experiences, together with a recognition of their significance. Proust's artistic calling and what might be called his spiritual calling are fulfilled through the same action: the writing of a novel of the most expansive and nuanced psychological acuity, whose climax both describes and elaborately explains the meaning of experiences of "the bliss of the Beyond" and freedom "from the order of time" that Proust himself enjoyed, and that he seeks through his literary art to evoke in responsive readers.[33] Proust's ultimate concerns may therefore be properly described as *aesthetic*, rather than *religious*, because for Proust—unlike for Eliot the Christian for whom, from the ultimate perspective on how one has lived, "[t]he poetry does not matter" (*EC* II, 71)—the *highest fulfillment* of spiritual obligation is the creation of an artwork that successfully conveys the truth of human experience in a way that evokes and affirms transcendent reality.

32 Proust, *The Guermantes Way*, III: 155; *Time Regained*, VI: 301.
33 Proust, *The Captive*, V: 347; *Time Regained*, VI: 264–65.

Selected Bibliography of Books about Proust

Albaret, Céleste. *Monsieur Proust*. Edited by Georges Belmont. Translated from the French by Barbara Bray. Reprinted with an introduction by André Alcimen. New York: New York Review of Books, 2003.

Alexander, Patrick. *Marcel Proust's Search for Lost Time: A Reader's Guide to The Remembrance of Things Past*. New York: Vintage Books, 2007.

Beckett, Samuel. *Proust*. New York: Grove Press, 1931. [Reprinted in Samuel Beckett. *Proust; and Three Dialogues with Georges Duthuit*. London: John Calder, 1965.]

Beistegui, Miguel de. *Proust as Philosopher: The Art of Metaphor*. Translated from the French by Dorothée Bonnigal Katz, with Simon Sparks and Miguel de Beistegui. London: Routledge, 2013.

Bersani, Leo. *Marcel Proust: The Fictions of Life and Art*. New York: Oxford University Press, 1965.

Bloch-Dano, Evelyne. *Madame Proust: A Biography*. Translated from the French by Alice Kaplan. Chicago: The University of Chicago Press, 2007.

Botton, Alain de. *How Proust Can Change Your Life*. New York: Vintage International Vintage Books, a Division of Random House, Inc., 1998.

Bowie, Malcolm. *Proust Among the Stars*. New York: Columbia University Press, 1998.

Brassaï, *Proust in the Power of Photography*. Translated by Richard Howard. Chicago: University of Chicago Press, 2001. [Originally published as *Marcel Proust sous l'emprise de la photographie*, text and photographs by Brassaï © Gilberte Brassaï and Éditions Galli-mard, 1997.]

Brée, Germaine. *Marcel Proust and Deliverance from Time.* Translated from the French by C. J. Richards and A. D. Truitt. New York: Grove Press, Inc., 1950, 1958.

Bucknall, Barbara J. *The Religion of Art in Proust.* Urbana: University of Illinois Press, 1969.

The Cambridge Companion to Proust. Edited by Richard Bales. Cambridge: Cambridge University Press, 2001.

Carson, Anne. *The Albertine Workout.* New York: New Directions Poetry Pamphlet #13, 2014.

Carter, William C. *Marcel Proust: A Life.* New Haven: Yale University Press, 2000.

Deleuze, Gilles. *Proust and Signs: The Complete Text.* Translated from the French by Richard Howard. London: The Athlone Press, 2000 [1964].

Karpeles, Eric. *Paintings in Proust: A Visual Companion to* In Search of Lost Time. London: Thames & Hudson, 2008.

Landy, Joshua. *Philosophy as Fiction: Self, Deception, and Knowledge in Proust.* New York: Oxford University Press, 2004.

March, Harold. *The Two Worlds of Marcel Proust.* New York: A. S. Barnes & Company, Inc., Perpetua Edition, 1961.

Moss, Howard. *The Magic Lantern of Marcel Proust: A Critical Study of Remembrance of Things Past.* Philadelphia: Paul Dry Books, 2012 [1962].

Muhlstein, Anka. *Monsieur Proust's Library.* New York: Other Press, 2012.

Painter, George D. *Marcel Proust: A Biography.* Revised and Enlarged Edition. Random House, London, Pimlico Imprint, 1996 [1959].

The Proust Project. Edited by André Aciman. New York: Farrar, Straus and Giroux, 2004.

Pugh, A. R. *The Birth of "À la recherche du temps perdu."* Lexington, KY: French Forum, 1987.

Shattuck, Roger. *Proust's Way: A Field Guide to* In Search of Lost Time. New York: W. W. Norton & Company, 2000.

Tadié, Jean-Yves. *Marcel Proust.* Translated from the French by Euon Cameron. New York: Viking, 2000.

White, Edmund. *Marcel Proust.* New York: Viking, 1999.

Contributors

Charles R. Embry, Ph.D. in Political Science, Duke University, is Professor Emeritus of Political Science at Texas A&M University-Commerce. A resident of Bellingham, Washington, he is the author of *The Philosopher and the Storyteller: Eric Voegelin and Twentieth-Century Literature* (University of Missouri Press) and most recently editor of *Voegelinian Readings of Modern Literature* (University of Missouri Press).

Michael Henry received his Ph.D. in 1974 from the University of Notre Dame where he studied with Gerhart Niemeyer and Eric Voegelin. Since 1977 he has taught philosophy at St. John's University in New York. He is also the Series Editor of the Library of Conservative Thought of Transaction Publishers. Recently, he edited a volume of the works of Niemeyer, *The Loss and Recovery of Truth* (St. Augustine's Press, 2013).

Glenn Hughes, Ph.D., is Professor of Philosophy at St. Mary's University in San Antonio, where he also holds the St. Mary's Chair in Catholic Philosophy. He is the author and editor of many philosophical and literary books and articles; his most recent book is *A More Beautiful Question: The Spiritual in Poetry and Art* (University of Missouri Press, 2011). With degrees in literature, history, and philosophy, he has been the recipient of numerous awards, including a 2008 Fulbright Scholar Grant to study at the Peace Research Institute of Oslo (PRIO).

Paulette Kidder is Associate Professor of Philosophy at Seattle University. She received her Ph.D. from Boston College in 1990. Dr. Kidder served as Associate Dean for Academic Affairs in the College of Arts and Sciences at Seattle University from 1999–2008, and as Interim

Dean from 2008–2009. She has published articles and presented at conferences on a range of subjects, including the philosophies of Martha Nussbaum, Eric Voegelin, Hans-Georg Gadamer, and Bernard Lonergan, S.J., as well as in the areas of feminism, health care ethics, philosophy and film, and philosophy and literature.

Thomas McPartland received a Ph.D. in intellectual history at the University of Washington in 1976. He was for many years director of the Whitney Young School of Honors and Liberal Studies at Kentucky State University, and has delivered numerous papers and published articles on Bernard Lonergan, and written two books on his thought, *Lonergan and the Philosophy of Historical Existence* and *Lonergan and Historiography: The Epistemological Philosophy of History.* He has made presentations for the American Political Science Association and at international conferences at Rome, Mainz, Germany, Toronto, Hong Kong, and Jerusalem. He was Kentucky State University Distinguished Professor of 2002–2003.

Index of Proper Names